All the Mortal Idols Abandoned

Brittney N Hamilton

WestBow
PRESS
A DIVISION OF THOMAS NELSON

WestBow Press books may be ordered through booksellers or by contacting:

WestBow Press
A Division of Thomas Nelson
1663 Liberty Drive
Bloomington, IN 47403
www.westbowpress.com
1-(866) 928-1240

Because of the dynamic nature of the Internet, any Web addresses or links contained in this book may have changed since publication and may no longer be valid. The views expressed in this work are solely those of the author and do not necessarily reflect the views of the publisher, and the publisher hereby disclaims any responsibility for them.

Scripture quotations marked NLT are taken from the Holy Bible, New Living Translation, copyright 1996, 2004. Used by permission of Tyndale House Publishers, Inc., Wheaton, Illinois 60189. All rights reserved.

Scripture taken from the New King James Version. Copyright 1979, 1980, 1982 by Thomas Nelson, inc. Used by permission. All rights reserved.

Scripture quotations marked (ESV) are from The Holy Bible, English Standard Version® (ESV®), copyright © 2001 by Crossway, a publishing ministry of Good News Publishers. Used by permission. All rights reserved.
Scripture taken from the HOLY BIBLE, NEW INTERNATIONAL VERSION®. Copyright © 1973, 1978, 1984 Biblica. Used by permission of Zondervan. All rights reserved.

Unless otherwise indicated all scripture came from the NIV.

ISBN: 978-1-4497-0397-4 (sc)
ISBN: 978-1-4497-0396-7 (dj)
ISBN: 978-1-4497-0479-7 (e)
Library of Congress Control Number: 2010939504
Printed in the United States of America

WestBow Press rev. date: 11/11/2010

Contents

Introduction to the Body

THE INVITATION

My Love,

I reach for you now as I always have. I want you to know that my loyalty was meant to hold up the stars forever. While it once hurt that, like time, you passed me by, it has now been made clear to you that I can take the stiff reins of your ride. I can give a helpful heart and show you those reins need to be let go so that the horses may find a new path. My embrace beckons for you like a lighthouse's light to the ship, piercing over dark-painted water with grace's melody. Just try to convince me that what or who you have is enough. Your inner parts writhe, exposing the realization that the territory that has been entered doesn't hold the supplies that your life needs. Don't pass me by for the rest of your life; I can only wait till your death. Look around at the invitations all around; found from My breath through the veined fingers of the trees to the decorated sunrise, being made known through your window. Consider these carefully detailed treasures instead of ignoring these worthy calls of genuinely innocent intentions, gliding from my direction.

My Ungraspable Love given,

The One holding you

Romans 7:3-4

A true believer is free in Jesus Christ. An illustration for marriage goes *'If [a woman's] husband dies, she is released from that law and is not an adulteress, even though she marries another man. So, my brothers, you also died to the law through the body of Christ, that you might belong to another, to him who was raised from the dead, in order that we might bear fruit to God' (Romans 7:3-4)*. The flesh strives to feed death and its master, Satan. By Jesus dying on the cross as a perfect sin offering, it forever replaced the old traditions or requirements and allows us who come to him to metaphorically nail the self that is rotten through and through to the cross.

Paul joyfully expresses, *"May I never boast except in the cross of our Lord Jesus Christ, through which the world has been crucified to me, and I to the world" (Galatians 6:14)*. When we give our lives to Him, the self, that had given into sin and had rejected the Father, (causing that separation that began with the disobedience in the garden, because of the serpent called sin) dies. This has allowed us to break sin's barrier and pardons us from judgment; the wrath of God.

Like in a marriage, the vow is, 'until death do us part.' Once one has died, the vow is obsolete and the other is free to either stay single or remarry. When we die to our old sinful nature, we are released from our former master. This is one who would think us nothing more than worthless. But when this master is removed from the authority that was given him originally by our will, we are made free. Now the former slaves are allowed to 'remarry' Jesus with no restraint, if they choose. If one is not willing to enter into an eternal relationship with the Holy One, he remains in the path of the hurricane of God's wrath.

Who would not want to take hold of freedom? *'If we have been united with him like this in his death, we will certainly also be united with him in his resurrection' (Romans 6:5)*. We are resurrected into light, where death can no longer affect us, because it is conquered by Jesus Christ, who lives in us. By him we are able to conquer death. We are conquerors and so much more!

THIS PROPHET'S OFFER

An opaque atmosphere of choking dust;
An arising symptom from it is a chill of emptiness.
You toss around the idea that maybe there is a clearing with a breath of freshness.
You consider fleeing, but don't know how to clear the air.
Bursting showers of pain,
You wish to erase the dance of past regrets,
to walk victorious through the dark, without shattering glass.
Up till now each piece has been further chipped by the lonely feet
of one single shadow full of worldly shame and fear.
You are lost.
I can see it.
I carry my hope from the clearing,
Love puppet's these hands that can reach down and pull you from this
lonely-echoing space.
I'll do my best to deter you from the gate of hell,
I hope to be used to save you from the pit of aimlessness.
Come away from her, the demons persuade,
They don't want you near holy flames.
The spiritual battle is intense,
 Existent to the discerned.
 Let the Author of Eternity pull you out of the pit of forever despair.
 The heart wasn't meant for artificial truths.
The demons play on your desires,
To persuade you that their direction is the only path;
With promises of revenge and all the pleasures one could count.
They don't mention that it is a manipulation
to pull one from the light that has now invaded the dark realm of your
flesh.
You don't want to play their games again,
You can't afford that gamble.
Welcome into the light.
Can you feel the genuine warmth,
traveling down in rays?

Their fingers run down your face, returning to color.
Finally, safe from the broad gate that leads to destruction.
Love surrounds you.
Remain in Him and you will be forever filled.

A Vision-Illustration

Christ hung on the cross, under a fading sky. On His side
shown the mark where the spear had struck the beautiful body
at one point. As the mark became focal point, the opening
that had poured out the stream of blood and water, unzipped.
It was like that of a zipper coming undone on a jacket. Inside
was a calm and peaceful path, leading to a narrow and sturdy
wooden gate. The gate hung open, always making known it's
welcome. The Narrow path and gate were there because
He Who is Greatest, came down from the thrown of heaven to
lead us there.

WHAT THE CROSS HAS DONE

Through Hosea, the word of the Lord promises *"I will ransom them from the power of the grave; I will redeem them from death. Where, O death, are your plagues? Where, O grave, is your destruction" (Hosea 13:14)?* This promise refers to the eventual remnant that would come and seek their life in the Lord.

With death, Satan could claim all, mastering all. A psalmist asks *"What man can live and not see death, or save himself from the power of the grave" (Psalms 89:48).* The exception to this was if the Spirit of God was in him or her. The great prophet Elijah had the spirit of God and was taken and did not taste death (Reference- 2 Kings 2:11). Elijah's story can be a shadow of what would result from the fulfillment of the Lord's promise; The Son suffering for us. This result is that through this plan, Christ The Son would go *"Ask the Father, and he will give you another Counselor to be with you forever—the Spirit of truth" (John 14:16-17).* Counselor (or Holy Spirit) being given, guarantees eternal life to all who come to and accepts, this token of sweet Father's sacrificial love.

In parables, Christ reveals ahead of time, the significance of the cross. He taught, *"When a strong man, fully armed, guards his own house, his possessions are safe. But when someone stronger attacks and overpowers him, he takes away the armor in which the man trusted and divides up the spoils" (Luke 11:21-22).* *"Or again, how can anyone enter a strong man's house and carry off his possessions unless he first ties up the strong man? Then he can rob his house" (Matthew 12:29).* Revealed here is the story of Satan with his greatest defense, death, until a greater power, the Son of God overpowers him. Christ is the promise fulfilled. Christ breaks through and holds the greatest victory ever, as death cowers at the fullness of the deity in Him. The Father is in Him because the Father is spirit. *"For in Christ, all the fullness of the deity lives in bodily form" (Colossians 2:9).* With the Creator fully in Him, there is nothing that can stand up against Him.

The Lord, who came down from His throne to reconcile us with our Creator, wanted to restore the relationship He once had with all in the beginning. The Lord also had His plan in mind to save us from His wrath. He taught us of His great, unorthodox ways and came to hold hands with, as well as eat meals with His children. The Creator came teaching us with authority, this plan to build the bridge of relationship with Him so that He may have a close bond with us and to offer safety from wrath. This plan was the crucifixion that would save us from death's mastering control of us, as well as the hurricane of wrath.

Taken were the 'keys' Satan had, his power to take all. Christ was pleased to bring back a key for each of us, being the power to overcome death as Christ had. Instead of being able to choose to take, Satan is reduced to only being able to try to persuade people to remain in his kingdom of dismay and aimlessness to feed death. It was as if sweet Jesus reached out His hand from death's prison cell and swapped the key ring! *"I am the Living One; I was dead, and behold I am alive for ever and ever! And I hold the keys of death and Hades" (Revelation 1:18).*

Gifts are given out of love, but it is the choice of the recipient whether to accept it or not. His true flock embraces this privilege to never have to taste death, to live forever in the presence of the Great Love. How wonderful! So, *"When we were controlled by the sinful nature, the sinful passions aroused by the law were at work in our bodies, so that we bore fruit for death. But now, by dying to what once bound us, we have been released from the law so that we serve in the new way of the Spirit, and not in the old way of the written code" (Romans 7:5-6).*

Newness of Life

TRANSFORMED BY RENEWAL

The Lord, our King, came from His throne to die for us who were less. There was no reason to have deserved such a gift. Christ had everything, yet He would leave it all to suffer for us who were drowning in our sin. For His faithful ones, He would grant newness of life. Newness of life, with its joys and the understanding that comes with obedience to Christ, is like no greatness this world can ever come close to offering. It is written, *"Do not conform any longer to the pattern of this world, but be transformed by the renewing of your mind" (Romans 12:2).*

In a movie titled Rigoletto, Romans 12:2 comes alive. The main character has been wounded in battle and allows the ugliness to flow and consume him. His war wound is like sin and shows how easy it can spread when one harbors and nurtures it, for freedom will dock elsewhere. As Paul warns, *'A little yeast works through the entire batch of dough' (Galatians 5:9).* Holding to the sinful nature leads only to destruction. The wound changes the once beloved man into a bitter and cruel person. The contamination overflows in the man.

Changes become evident following the title character's search for a pure heart. He finds a young woman named Bonnie, who is upright and, in his eyes, pure in all her ways. Her acceptance of him and her actions begin to transform him, removing the hate and ugliness. Now changed, Rigoletto saves someone who is dear to Bonnie and it costs him his life. He learns to care for someone other than himself. He picks up pieces of Bonnie's goodness.

Our story is parallel to Rigoletto's. Covered with ugly scars of sin, we are found and can choose to begin a relationship with the Father. With the Father's love, acceptance, and His Spirit placed in us, we are transformed, becoming a new creation. When entered into the family of God, we are forgiven and the scarlet sin is scrubbed away. We nail sin to the cross and are separated from it as far as the opposite end of the earth. We are separated from sin and raised in righteousness by my Beloved's grace, not meant to return to decay.

The Father can work through us and find others who thirst for newness of life when we begin living out our faith, as Rigoletto displayed when saving Bonnie's friend from drowning. In his case, "the great love [he] has shown proves that [his] many sins are forgiven" , speaks for him. Matching faith with deeds allows sweet Father to illuminate us to others. Jesus' brother James writes, *'Faith by itself, if it is not accompanied by action, is dead'* *(James 2:17)*. In the gospels, Christ's words match His actions. The apostle Peter asks Jesus how many times he should forgive his brother and Peter suggests seven times. In response, Jesus answers *"I tell you, not seven times, but seventy-seven times" (Matthew 18:22)*. With His friends (us), Jesus forgives sin after sin, as He had with the Israelites who constantly turned away.

My dad wrote a poem about what happens when a town is abandoned. The verse that I found to have significance is 'to leave it all will lead you home'. As described in what happens to worldly things, they all erode, fade, and become totally useless. Before becoming a new creation, one's life is faded, erosive, and useless. But leaving that life of disrepair and being transformed by renewal is to find life and ultimately lead one to the unimaginably wonderful home in eternity!

We have been blessed beyond the curse and the Father should be praised every day and hour because of his generosity. He didn't have to spread his love over us. He could ignore us and turn His face from us, but He wanted to give His love away because His Love is uncontainable. Given an invitation, Christ will break any barrier and help any one of us Rigolettos be transformed by renewal!

RENEWAL

The mountains call an icy blue wind to their snowy tops.
With a freshly powdered landscape, everything is white.
While many surrender to some wintry feet,
the pines stand triumphantly against a chilling shield.
The recently clear whisper of the lake says farewell
as it is imprisoned by still-so-thin ice
that may catch it's prey if anyone dares to step foot on it.
But so powerful are the affects of spring on the snow front,
a new painting is created with young color.
The heaven up above patches the overjoyed sky with petal pink clouds,
underlined with a stream of majestic purple.
Salmon and gentle blue slide in and the sky is a pastel rainbow.
The still lake breaks free from the icy shell
and paints a picture of the sky to lie on its clean surface.
Green is thrown back into the scene,
as newborn grass pushes through the sun warmed ground.
Overjoyed trees fan out their schools of leaves
and regain their special coat from God.

SIGNIFICANCE-SMALL ISN'T A WORD

Evidence is found that shows that the Great Love is not one to overlook a child who calls on Him; never thinking he is unworthy of rescue. Sweet Christ teaches of the parable of the lost sheep, in response to comments made about Him eating with sinful men. The parable reveals the faithful and caring nature of The Father. It goes that there is a flock of sheep on a hill, but one wanders off, so the Shepherd searches for it. He leaves the other ninety-nine on the hill. The Shepherd is more excited about finding the sheep that has run off than about the ones who haven't.

Eventually, during Jesus' long chain of miracles, He and the apostles sail to a region of the Gerasenes, where one (or two, depends on the gospel being read) violent, demon-possessed men are roaming. (Jesus had mentioned in John, that he does what the Father does, so the Holy Spirit led him there.) After Jesus has driven the demons out, making the men free, reports of the miracle flood the area. Unfortunately, not all people embrace the wonder of this miracle. The people of the nearby town are frightened by the marvelous thing Christ has done. As a result, the town's people beg Jesus to leave; therefore he isn't able to do any other business there. The point that even though only two were there to receive the mercy of beautiful Christ, and there were many other areas that Jesus had accomplished more in, Jesus still took the time to release these men from captivity. Even when there are few, the Lord will not disregard them.

In Abraham's time, the cities of greatest wickedness in the eyes of the Lord were unknowingly standing at the edge of being wiped out by God's hand, yet Abraham inquired about what might save any upright seekers of God in them. Abraham approached the Father boldly, as he questioned that if there were fifty to as little as ten in all in the cities, if the Lord would spare them for those few. My Lord affirmed that they would not come to destruction if any righteous people were found; otherwise the cities were as good as demolished. Each one who eagerly seeks out the Lord of all will not be over-looked; they will be overwhelmed by the love that enfolds them. *"For the Lord loves the just and will not forsake his faithful ones" (Psalms 37:28).*

One is also never too small and insignificant to play a part in Love's plan. Forget how you were viewed in the world in relation to fame, title, success, etc. *"God does not look at the things man looks at, man looks at the outward appearance but God looks at the heart" (1 Samuel 16:7).*

At the time of Christ's birth, the angel of the Lord appeared to humble shepherds in the field. They were the first to see my Christ (apart from Mary and Joseph) as well as the first ones to go out and spread news about the gospel and the virgin mother. Truly the bible is filled from beginning to end with simple and humble people who were not too small to play a role in the Father's story. From fishermen who became apostles of Christ, to a prostitute who was cooperative in helping men on a mission, to a boy with a stone and a sling protecting an entire army, to a demon-possessed man from the tombs who later witnessed to his town, to a man born under slavery who would help deliver the nation of Israel, to name a few. Whatever you are for the world is meaningless, what you can be for the Father of Love is what is significant!

The small can add up. Even when an act of obedience to Christ seems so small, it can truly be great in the eyes of the Lord. Consider a faucet that is dripping; each small drop adds to the puddle, eventually filling a whole cup with water. It becomes a full glass if one is patient and it refreshes the one who drinks it. In the same way every effort I make or every time I obey the Lord's will it can add up and complete God's plan in my life. Each of our small acts can cause a big change. Each of our faith can contribute, considering we all match faith with deeds, to show shadows of little pieces of the kingdom of heaven down here on earth.

No Looking Back

In the book of Matthew, Jesus informs the apostles that *"When they see standing in the holy place 'the abomination that causes desolation; spoken of through the prophet Daniel-then let those in Judea flee to the mountains. Let no one on the roof of his house go down to take anything out of the house. Let no one in the field go back to get his cloak" (Matthew 24:15-18)*. If the Lord is calling or commanding, yet someone is unable to part with the ways of the world and what it offers, or the past, then they are holding on to worthless and perishable things. They are grasping lifelessness. If he or she is making the Father wait, this could be a sign of idolatry, where the Lord isn't the priority. Holding to the world is holding to the past that we were cut from. *"The man who loves his life will lose it, while the man who hates his life in this world will keep it for eternal life" (John 12:25)*.

When the Lord had planned the destruction of Sodom and Gomorrah, He instructed Lot and his family to flee and not look back. He wanted them to move forward. *"But Lot's wife looked back and she became a pillar of salt' (Genesis 19:26)*. While she started off moving forward to the Lord's call, she was holding on to the superficial life in the city of destruction. It cost her everything and she never finished the race God had set before her.

The mention of Lot's wife reveals the foolishness and hindrance of holding to what is over or destined to dissolve, because it is a blockade between us and the Father. In a letter, John writes, *"Do not love the world or anything in the world. If anyone loves the world, the love of the Father is not in him. For everything in the world—the cravings of sinful man, the lust of his eyes and the boasting of what he has and does—comes not from the Father but from the world. The world and its desires pass away, but the man who does the will of God lives forever" (1 John 2:15-17)*.

Perhaps Lot's wife wasn't fully devoted to The Father's plan. Not having full devotion to The Father's instruction is only being half-hearted, or lukewarm. Christ addresses a lukewarm attitude by saying to the church in Laodicea, *"I know your deeds, that you are neither cold nor hot. I wish you were either one or the other! So, because you are lukewarm—neither hot nor cold—I am about to spit you out of my mouth. You say, 'I am rich; I have acquired wealth and do not need a thing.' But you do not realize that you are wretched, pitiful, poor, blind and naked" (Revelation 3:15-17)*. From what Christ expresses here, a lukewarm attitude is not what He is looking for in His harvest field. He shares that *'No one who puts his hand to the plow and looks back is fit for service in the kingdom of God" (Luke 9:62).* Are we willing to let go of what is behind and work on a new plot of land?

Christ taught that *"no one sews a patch of unshrunk cloth on an old garment. If he does, the new piece will pull away from the old, making the tear worse. And no one pours new wine into old wineskins. If he does, the wine will burst the skins and both the wine and the wineskins will be ruined. No, he pours new wine into new wineskins" (Mark 2:21-22).* This parable is metaphorical for showing the importance of pouring **all** efforts into a new beginning [life] instead of former ways. This parable visibly suggests that it is of no use to continue focusing on the past and the old decayed life. It wastes time, energy and effort to dwell on what is no longer here. Jump whole-heartedly into following the Father into the spiritual. Ride into the future. Through Isaiah, it is warned to *"Forget the former things; do not dwell on the past. See I am doing a new thing! Now it springs up; do you not perceive it?' (Isaiah 43:18-19).* If we keep looking back and delaying on the fresh, how can we see what the Lord is doing new or next in our lives?

Overjoyed by this Restoration

The breeze feels genuine as it never has, as does this untamed star of the
day.
I've missed you, my love, like only you can imagine;
Infinite pale moons that cannot light intensely enough,
a thousand whispers could not join together to make the perfect
description.
A tornado could ravage in my soul and touch but an edge of it compared
to the desire to find you, Lord.
So decorated is this warmth to my senses, that it could write the
unimaginable into life and melt appalling figures into the nothingness
that dares not re-invent itself

LOVE INHALED

Love, real love will find its way in the densest jungle;
across the most rocky path with a no shoes sign.
The ungraspable, non liquefied substance the heart runs dry without.
Your love, oh Lord finds me and pulls out strength;
Finding me and being my strength through a weakness.
It embraces me with words never truly spoken to me before.
The Love always pours into me the song of pure and innocent thoughts,
 That drowns out the unholy temptations that prowl like a predator all
around this land that I'm an alien to.
Rejection is forever lost;
It is banished to a labyrinth with an exit always moving.
Significance lights itself in a way it couldn't previously dream of being
lit.
Fear drowns in this light, unable to swim since it can't take the strength
of the waves.
I sense that I am going to make it;
A climb up, through what has been my fall.
A beautiful new motion is carried with mercy and its wings are streaked
with grace.

FORGIVENESS

There is an amazing power that I had never believed in before....the power of forgiveness. I used to hate the word because I associated it with being weak and letting people walk all over me. That was before God allowed me to see the truth and let me tell you, God's truths are **_so_** much different than the world's 'artificial' truths. God showed me that I wasn't protecting myself when I wasn't forgiving. Instead, Satan's lie had placed a dark veil over my eyes. By not forgiving, I was actually making myself the person that I was trying to avoid in the first place.

After being in a 'desert wander' for a few years, I thought the ability to love others was beginning to fade. Because of the enduring hope I held and one long argument with Him, God grabbed the edge of that door and just threw it back open! He had been waiting there all along, saying "I'm always here, my love!" After that, He began revealing to me many fallacies that had engulfed me previously; when I wasn't as mature in my walk. One of the first truths He revealed for me to learn was that forgiveness is a good thing because it welcomes joy, maturity, and His freedom. He has called us to forgive; *"for if you forgive men when they sin against you, your heavenly Father will also forgive you. But if you do not forgive men their sins, your Father will not forgive your sins" (Matthew 6: 14-15).*

You see, when we don't forgive it opens the way for resentment and we are not able to move towards being Christ-like. Resentment is anger. Anger leads to hate and loss of trust; it creates a chain of feelings that tie one down from moving towards the Lord. Before God spoke about this truth, I hadn't realized that I was allowing these dark feelings to flow inside because of people that I chose not to forgive. My earthly father especially, caused the majority of my resentment. I had hungered for some of his time. I hated that he lied to me to the point where I stopped taking him seriously. How about all he said he would do and never did? No one had ever hurt me more than this father had, yet I was holding on. It kept me so weighed down. God helped me forgive him and WOW! When I gave it to the Him, the Lord broke those chains into nothing but links on the ground. The people I hadn't been able to forgive couldn't hurt me anymore! I tasted some genuine freedom there. I felt so light. THAT is the POWER of forgiveness in GOD's truth!

All the Mortal Statues Hidden/ The Door

Freeing winds of change are complimenting a canvas of golden sky.
 Drops in the ocean splash up like glitter lined hands.
They rise up toward clouds that are rippled like the desert sand.
All the mortal statues are hidden....
The statues' faces can no longer be seen,
as the exposing power of day unveils their deception and intimidating presence.
Though at night the cool moon scans over them through the trees,
and the giant faces bring dread,
staring down at me as I run through.
Rays of moonlight fall around me;
bathing patches of forest in purity.
Though at first, I don't notice them,
 for my fear distracts me from those rays' safe, rumbling calls of guidance
Then a mighty door ahead, which nothing can shadow,
And no hinges or frames can support,
opens as a beacon to me like the ship's welcome home by a lighthouse.
Gold spills out and infects the area, crawling across the forest floor and up the nearby trees.
Still I run past the giant figures that mock and try to persuade me to stand helpless,
The door is open as the trees hide the moon's light;
causing the mortal statues to again be hidden from view.
Embraced by the door's light, it pulls me in.
Coming through feels like nothing else could;
like metamorphosis; like undisturbed peace; like rejoicing at my arrival to my home shore.
It's like dancing in the breath of most tender comfort.
The mortal statues are left at my back, I fear them no more.
I have fallen in love with the man inside;
the Creator of the door.

Metaphorical for The Lord bringing me through troubled times, this is inspired by a favorite scriptural verse of mine. In Isaiah, it is written,

'Whether you turn to the right or to the left, your ears will hear a voice behind you saying this is the way, walk in it' (Isaiah 30:21). He is always calling and waiting for us to notice him; 'rays bathing forest in purity' is symbolic of this. When we do obey Christ, we help our relationship with Him; we are able to draw nearer to Him. Sometimes things like fear and doubt, or our 'mortal statues', are played on us and choke out the Father. It is us who leave the pen; a shepherd does not leave the sheep, the sheep are the ones that run away. Christ never leaves us and is always willing to guide us in the ways we should go. Through Jesus Christ, the creator of the door to salvation, (who is the door himself), we have been enabled to draw near and may cross into his unequalled light.

CHAIN REACTION

Without the Law, there is no consciousness of sin; without consciousness
of sin, there is no
Repentance
If no repentance, no relationship with God
If no relationship with God, no grace or mercy accepted

Opposite of a Worldly Mindset

Do not think the Way They Think- Colossians 2:20-23

Believers are strangers in a strange land. We are foreigners who follow a true light and live on a sacred ground, where we believe in a great force that falls around us like a shower of sun rays. The Truth, who called me His before I was able to love, has promised to remain true if I remain under His wings of cover. Now if I have such an overwhelming and comforting strength inside and around me, why should I fear what the worldly do?

The Apostle Paul asks such a question. Addressing the Colossians in a letter, he reasons, *"Since you died with Christ to the basic principles of this world, why, as though you still belonged to it, do you submit to its rules: 'Do not handle! Do not taste! Do not touch!'"? These are all destined to perish with use, because they are based on human commands and teachings"* (Colossians *2:20-23).* By thinking this way, the Colossians must have been in doubt or underestimated the protection and strength of Christ.

Paul asks *'why, as though you still belong to [the world] do you submit to its rules: Do not handle! Do not taste! Do not touch!' (20-21)?* This reminds me of a recent example. A recent flu virus has been going around that has many taking on sanitation craze and has adjusted their behavior with great caution measures and such, for fear. At work, I have seen such sights as a family with young children. Each child wearing oversized medical gloves. Paul encourages to *'eat anything sold in the meat market without raising questions of conscience, for, "The earth is the Lord's, and everything in it"* (*¹ Corinthians 10:25-26).* Even if plagues/chaos is around us, will the remnant be struck by it if it is God's wrath? Certainly not!

The book of Acts follows Paul on a journey to spread the gospel, at one point being on an island where a toxic snake attacks Paul. He is never affected. Neither him nor us have to live in fear, because has not God said that He will *'revive me: [he] shall stretch forth [his] hand against the wrath of my enemies, and [his] right hand shall save me' (Psalm 138:7).*

Do not fear, for in Revelation 7, all plagues of wrath are held back by angels at the four corners. They are held back until God's children are sealed with the Holy Spirit, given as a deposit. Also, consider the first Passover, in Moses' days, where the plague of death passed by all who had the blood of a Lamb.

He or she who believes and shower's in the remedial blood of Him who is Greatest, is like being shielded in a protective finish. A powerful Psalm goes like this, *"You will not fear the terror of night nor the arrow that flies by day, nor the pestilence that stalks in the darkness, nor the plague that destroys at midday. A thousand may fall at your side, ten thousand at your right hand. But it will not come near you. You will only observe with your eyes and see the punishment of the wicked. If you make the Most High your dwelling-even the Lord, who is my refuge- then no harm will befall you, no disaster will come near your tent' (Psalms 91:5-10)* . This whole psalm is powerful in telling of Savior's protection and I encourage one to read it as a whole.

The prophet Isaiah records, *"The LORD spoke to me with his strong hand upon me, warning me not to follow the way of this people. He said: Do not call conspiracy everything that these people call conspiracy; do not fear what they fear, and do not dread it. The LORD Almighty is the one you are to regard as holy, he is the one you are to fear, he is the one you are to dread, and he will be a sanctuary" (Isaiah 8:11-14)*. You and I are free being in Him and free from the regulations and customs of the world. Yet, while this is so, we should maintain a wise mindset and not treat foolishly with testing, the protection that is ours. Keep in mind what is for the good of the Kingdom.

Paul's questioning to the Colossians is also saying that <u>we need to do what is right</u> even when it's not a 'normal' act at the world's standards. We are not limited or trapped, Praise you Father!

So what can this world do to us that we need to live in fear or in the mindset of the worldly? As proved in these various places as well as others in the bible, the Father will take care of His treasured ones. Past, present, and future, we are protected. He is also not one to parallel His plans with the mindset of the world. Those beings so, let's not allow ourselves to be contained by living by the standards of this world. Rather, do what the Father desires, even if it means standing out. There is nothing wrong with that. _

MATTHEW 5:29-30

In the Gospels, sweet Jesus instructed *"If your right eye causes you to sin, gouge it out and throw it away. It is better for you to lose one part of your body than for your whole body to be thrown into hell. And if your right hand causes you to sin, cut it off and throw it away, It is better for you to lose one part of your body than for your whole body to go to hell"* (Matthew 5:29-30). This teaching is included when Jesus is talking about the topic of Lust, which causes one to break His law. It contaminates the body, because it causes one to have committed Adultery in mind.

Jesus didn't mean literally to dismember oneself, but rather the feelings and behavior that could ruin everything that does not agree with Christ. The old ways, when the flesh was the controlling force, are not good for representing Christ.

An old way that needed to be cut off from me was anger. This anger would make me think all sorts of evil thoughts. It is similar to yeast, where just a small amount is needed to work through the whole batch. The evil thoughts by themselves are already distasteful to God, so one is guilty even before the whole is baked. These sinful attitudes and such, if retained, works into the self until it takes over and makes up the person.

Paul writes *'Get rid of the old yeast that you may be a new batch without yeast—as you really are. For Christ, our Passover lamb, has been sacrificed'* (1 Corinthians 5:7). The polluted thoughts have to be mastered and not allowed to master us. These are possible to control because Jesus tells the parable using human actions, commanding to "cut it off" and "gouge it out". My Beloved said it was our choice or, more accurately, a command for a child of God. Of course, a child does not have to pull it alone. Christ can and will help. *"Ask and it will be given to you"* (Matthew 7:7). If something is in agreement with His will, then it will be given.

One must ask for and develop <u>self-control.</u> Christ, as well as others in the New Testament, instructs to have this discipline. The definition for self-control is restraint exercised over one's own impulses, desires, or emotions; temperance. Christ states, *"Therefore, if your whole body if full of light and no part of it dark, it will be completely lighted, as when the light of a lamp shines on you"* (Luke 11:36). Get rid of the contamination sources that dim the rays, and see how the light overtakes you and makes you shine like Christ!

Tame the tongue by watching what you say and praying about self-control. The tongue is a world of evil. *"Out of the same mouth come praise and cursing. My brothers, this should not be. Can both fresh water and saltwater flow from the same spring"* (James 3:10-11)? How can Christ's body have fires of evil? Jesus is the Holy one and we are his body. We strive to be like Him.

Out With Impurity

Impurity is corrupting the Holy Spirit's dwelling. Paul mentions *"The body is not meant for sexual immorality, but for the Lord, and the Lord for the body" (1 Corinthians 6: 13)*. Also, he asks *"Do you not know that your bodies are members of Christ himself? Shall I then take the members of Christ and unite them with a prostitute" (1 Corinthians 6:15)?* One does not want to join with a prostitute because it is written *'the two will become one flesh' (Mark 10:6)*. Consider that if we are the bride and the body of Christ and some are impure or sexually immoral, it is as if Christ is being united with an unfaithful love. Being the body, this even makes his body impure. If we have reverent fear of the Lord, we wouldn't dare allow that to be. We know that giving Christ a corrupted name and image is an undeserved insult. Christ deserves respect, for He beckons us to use Him as the exit from the pure catastrophe that surrounds on all sides; that watches to digest us.

A true relationship is bonded by love in every crevice. As the bride of Christ, who were called and first loved by him, we should be taken by an urge to love Him in return. We ought to be taken by a desire to show Christ gratitude for what He has done and is always doing for us. He has done it all because of His great love for us.

In a relationship, being unfaithful is not living in truth. As written, *"Love does not delight in evil but rejoices with the truth" (1 Corinthians 13:6)*. Walking in the Light, can we possibly desire to be unfaithful or doing anything that is not of the truth? The Spirit cannot desire to corrupt the Lord. Who could reject Christ's overwhelming love?

Another reason to keep the body pure is if one takes good care of the body, he or she can be trusted with more someday in eternity. If one can't take good care of what they have been given in this life, why should she be trusted with more in eternity? In the parable of the talents, the third man acted foolishly with what he was given to take care of. Because of his poor choices, it cost him both the respect and trust of the master, as well as what he had been entrusted with (*Reference Matthew 25*). If one wants more and greater things, they must learn to take care of the lesser things first. What is done in one's current life will effect what is gained or sown in eternity.

THE HARVEST OF THE WHEAT AND WEEDS (MATTHEW 13:24-28)

To teach about His kingdom, Christ reveals this parable; *"The kingdom of heaven is like a man who sowed good seed in his field. But, while everyone was sleeping, his enemy came and sowed weeds among the wheat and went away. When the wheat sprouted and formed heads, the weeds also appeared. The owner's servants came to him and said, "Sir, didn't you sow good seeds in your field? Where then did the weeds come from?" "An enemy did this," he replied'* (Matthew 13:24-28). The servant asks if they should pull out the weeds, but the master said do not because they might pull the wheat out as well. Instead the servant should wait for the harvest and then separate.

We all began in the image of the Everlasting Father (Genesis), who has shined on us with His love. Love is given freely and does not control, but allows one to learn from experience. God has allowed us to make choices and choose the path we want to go. Some were predestined and go on the Narrow path that leads to life, while others choose the broad highway.

The broad highway screams death and evil, but the many who travel it either do not hear of another choice or do not heed screams that warn of death. As in the parable of the four soils, recorded in three of the gospels (Matthew 13, Mark 4: 1-9, and Luke 8:4-8) they are the seeds that are eaten. Other seeds, resulting in weeds, are ones choked out by worldly matters. There are ones who are driven away by persecution. Only half-hearted and selective, they want only the easy way. They become weeds.

The full weight must be bore when taking up crosses. Travelling down the narrow path makes sense to the ones who hold that weight, because an inheritance waits at the end. The inheritors of the new earth are the useful and valued crop of the current Earth. Wheat provides food for others, is usually bought at a price, and when a draught or poor growth of it comes, people are negatively effected.

At the resurrection, the angels will separate the righteous from the evildoing rebels. Some fall onto the cold and rusted grounds of eternal punishment, and others into the warmest embrace ever to be found; eternal life. Travelling the narrow suits his or her taste for adventure.

Now in regard to the enemy who sows the weeds in; Satan sneaks around creating sin where he goes. *"Sin is not taken into account when the Law is not present"* (Romans 5:13). The Law exposes Satan's plan. *"Therefore, just as sin entered the world through one man, and death through sin, and in the way death came to all men, because all sinned' (Romans 5:12).*

When the good news of Christ is revealed, some turn away from sin, dying to it. It is nailed to the cross that saves the inheritors. In turn they are not mastered by death, since death comes through sin. This is how the wheat is able to be separated from the weeds. A better future awaits those who choose to be the valued crop, thanks to the Lord our God!

Unwise Destructions

Once, when digging through an old 'memory box' in the basement once, someone very close to me found a slip of paper that would alter her way of thinking. The paper revealed that that her parents had had an abortion before she had been born. Only a few years after the abortion, she had entered the family. This old friend had previously been accepting of the right of abortion, since it was a 'right' of the mother and hadn't affected her life in particular. She also considered the prospective of those who, by being unwillingly violated, had become pregnant. After discovering what her parents had done, she was struck with thoughts of what ifs. "What if I had been the one conceived first and then aborted. What if I had been aborted as well as the previous?" These questions disturbed her, but upon meditating on her faith, found shelter under a cover of thankfulness that the Lord had allowed her to live. She was thankful for a beautiful love story that was hers in the arms of her soul's lover, Jesus. She was thankful for a purpose that she could fulfill, offering to other's lives the invitation of the cup of living water she had been offered. The salvation she had accepted. What glory she would be able bring our Lord!

Abortion is so important to prevent because, believer or not, all are the Lord's creation. We were made to be a dwelling place of the Holy Spirit. We are created to be built as God's temple. Abortion, involves a young life who's *'angels in heaven always see the face of my Father in heaven"* (Matthew 18:10). What if in his or her future, this life chooses to follow Christ? They might enter a situation where they are the only one who can influence a certain person. His or her absence can have a negative impact in these situations. As Christ observes, *"The harvest is plentiful, but the workers are few. Ask the Lord of the harvest, therefore to send out workers into the harvest field" (Matthew 9:37-38).* Why Christ felt He needed to mention this is because many are lost and in need of His guiding light. They are available and could be waiting for someone to be sent into their lives and help assist them out of the sinister cave of chaos. Many lives haven't been given the choice of life or death. The conquerors the Lord Jesus can only touch so many, which are the ones in our realm of influence. To send out more workers will better cover more ground, so to say. More workers will better guarantee that everyone is being reached.

One of many other actions to encourage prevention of is suicide. In Isaiah, it is written *"Woe to him who quarrels with his Maker, to him who is but a potsherd among the potsherds on the ground. Does the clay say to the* potter, 'What are you making?' Does your work say, 'He has no hands' (Isaiah 45:9-10)? We need to respect ourselves because the creator should not be critiqued or disrespected on his creation. 'Shall what is formed say to him who formed it, "He did not make me"? Can the pot say of the potter, "He knows nothing" (Isaiah 29:16)?' If he has made us, how can we say that Him who is greatest, has made a mistake? Suicide results in damnation because one is attempting to sit on The Father's chair and override what the Father knows is best with what the person believes is better.

THE YEAST OF THE PHARISEES'- SPIRITUAL SIGHT

In the Gospels, Christ Jesus warns the disciples to watch out for the 'yeast of the Pharisees.' They think this mean literally the rise-assisting ingredient used in bread. It is used metaphorically and in spiritual terms. An interpretation of the negative 'yeast' is the idea of having spiritual blindness. Some of the Pharisees *come near to [God] with their mouth and honor [him] with their lips, but their hearts are far from [him]. Their worship of [God] is made up only of rules taught by men* (Isaiah 29:13). They were so wrapped up in the traditions of men and the old Covenant that they could not accept Jesus, the son of God and the introduction of the new Covenant. They were so focused on traditions passed down by man that they couldn't hear God in the now. If a miraculous thing or sign happened and it didn't agree with the tradition, even if it was truly from God they wouldn't accept it. The Pharisees, along with other people of Israel were probably expecting someone opposite of Christ. They probably expected someone who was wealthy and in armor.

As recorded in the gospel of John, a man born blind has his sight restored when Jesus spreads a mud and saliva mixture over his eyes and has him wash it off in the Pool of Salome. However, the opposing Pharisees state (concerning the Lord) *"This man is not from God, for he does not keep the Sabbath"* (John 9:16). A miracle has taken place, yet the focal point of these Pharisees is that their own traditions are not kept. They are spiritually blind and fail to discern truth. They are walking in the flesh and have not seen what is happening in the spiritual. If they truly knew The Most High, they would have recognized Jesus. They did not. As Jesus morbidly states, *"Where a dead body is, there the vultures will gather"* (Luke 17:37). He is referring to those who can see in the spiritual. The spirit will lead them in all truth. The Lord's Spirit will discern things in the spiritual realm.

In the Old Testament, spiritual blindness is evident in the story of a corrupted prophet named Balaam. Balaam had been summoned by Balak, King of Moab, to curse a people who were blessed by the Lord. The Lord commanded Balaam not to do so. The Lord also commanded Balaam not to go with the princes (sent from Balak), who bribed him with worldly riches. The second time princes were sent, God allowed Balaam to go. While Balaam obeyed these commands, he was operating in the wrong realm for following God. Scriptures reveal that *'God was very angry when [Balaam] went, and the angel of the LORD stood in the road to oppose him'* (Numbers 22:22). Balaam was not operating in the spiritual, or he would have seen the angel ready to stop him. Perhaps he had his mind set on the worldly riches promised by the Moabites. His donkey saw the angel and tried to stop, but in response, Balaam beat her. He did this because he failed to see how God was working. When the Lord gave him spiritual sight, he was able to see the angel was opposing him. The angel stated, *"I have come here to oppose you because your path is a reckless one before me. The donkey saw me and turned away from me these three times. If she had not turned away, I would certainly have killed you by now, but I would have spared her"* (Numbers 22:32-33). Metaphorically, this shows that we cannot move to do the Lord's will when we cannot see what His will is. Jesus informs, *"Your eye is the lamp of your body. When your eyes are good, your whole body also is full of light. But when they are bad, your body also is full of darkness. See to it, then, that the light within you is not darkness"* (Luke 11:34-35). To see what He desires, we must have spiritual sight.

Someone once told me, after reading a certain book series, that the ones who came to preach (in the books) were not the best dressed or the greatest looking. They were humble in appearance. I am reminded of this when thinking of John the Baptist. The gospels describe his outward appearance and diet saying, *'[John] wore clothing made of camels' hair, with a leather belt around his waist and he ate locust and wild honey'* (Mark 1:6). He was not so focused on the outward appearance and putting on a display for others' praising opinions, but for his precious mission. Being humble in the way he looked can be seen metaphorically. With John, this simplicity might have made him less physically attractive and desirable; less on having others admiring his looks or wanting to be around him for what he might have had (ex- nice clothes, friend for personal benefit, and popularity). It allowed the people to focus less on what is seen and more on what is unseen._ After all *'we walk by faith not by sight'* (2 Corinthians 5:7 KJV).

Jesus rightly states that life is more than food and the body more than clothes. If a person is judged based on worldly standards, they are being judged unfairly. Outward appearance is looking in the worldly realm, but the spiritual vision sees the mark of truth, the Father. *"Stop judging by mere appearances, and make a right judgment"* (John 7:24). In this context, Jesus is calling for the people to not judge people based on physical appearances, nor for everything they know little about. Make right decisions on what is true.

Another type of 'yeast' Christ discussed with the disciples. One should not get caught up in the act of hypocrisy. If hypocrisy or anything else that does not belong in Christ's body gets mixed in or becomes a part of one's behavior, it will become hard to detect. This detestable habit can contaminate the whole self, preventing one from realizing that there is 'a plank' in his own eye. As Jesus shares, if one wants to take the speck out of his brother's eye, he must first remove the plank from his own eye. This will avoid hypocrisy. We must first examine ourselves before we can offer help to others. Practice what your tongue is preaching. Respect comes with others seeing the practices you speak of in your life and creating real fruit.

PLACING THE HEART IN HEAVEN

An enjoyable band of mine sings as the chorus to a song,
"What you have. What you want. What you need, gonna be your savior"
I was singing these words and I think about the lesson in the Bible that
lights that where one's treasure is, there their heart will be also. So, If I
place or store my treasures in heaven (where age and rust can't affect it,
and thieves can't break in and steal), which is not seeking worldly praise
and acceptance, my heart will dwell there in my Father's kingdom.

Having a True and Great Faith

HOPE FOR AN AMAZING FAITH

If Jesus had come for the first time on earth around this time period and walked among us with the message of life, I would have kneeled at his feet in wonder. When He looked into my eyes, I would hope to amaze Him with great faith and love. I would hope my faith would mirror the type of true faith that Christ would have spoken of to the ones who would come to learn from Him. This is the true faith that Christ speaks to all who come to take His yoke upon them and learn.

Jesus' teaching, the faith like a mustard seed, says this seed is the smallest of all, but becomes one of the largest of garden plants; large enough for the birds to perch in its shade. He mentioned that if one has faith as small as a mustard seed, he can say to the mulberry tree to uproot itself and replant in the sea and it will be done (Read Luke 17:6). Whatever is done for the will of Christ will be done. One has to make sure that they have complete faith that it can be done, without doubt.

In the Word, there are some wonderful portrayals of individuals who amazed Christ with their great faith. The centurion and the woman with a demon-possessed daughter, as introduced in the gospels, were two who possessed a faith that pleased and continues to please Him.

The centurion was a Roman officer who was despised by the Jews because the Romans were in control. Despite this, he humbled himself to put in a request to the Lord. He put aside the fact that he had a high rank and people he commanded below him. **Being humble is a ground for strengthening faith.** This centurion requested that a paralyzed servant of his be healed. He wanted the healing so greatly and believed so strongly in the faith he possessed that the world's standards couldn't infect to stop him. The centurion's faith did not only include humility, but in caring for the servant, was also fulfilling one of the greatest commandments (Read Luke 10:25-37). As written, a follower of Christ should 'love his or her neighbor as themselves. With his faith, the solder showed compassion and sought help for his 'neighbor', this servant whom he cared about and wanted healed. It was for the servant that the centurion pushed aside his status to get help for. Aside from not being doubtful, we have seen some strong attitudes in this testimony. **Humility and loving others** help make up an amazing faith.

A Canaanite woman came to Jesus in the region of Tyre and Sidon with a request that her demon-possessed child be healed. Now to the Jews, the Canaanites were pagans who had little, if any, chance to be saved. Sources claim that the term 'dog' was used in this culture by the Jews. The term was to insult those of the woman's nation as well as those from other nations. Jesus uses the term when responding to the request but not to insult her. Perhaps He was testing her. Her response to Him shows that she was willing to be insulted for a blessing. Metaphorically, she was willing to suffer for her faith. Perhaps revealing this devotion of suffering for her faith was the reason for Christ testing her with this term. To be an example to all the followers who were standing near. Looking at this testimony, a strong faith requires following Christ not only through peace, but also through sufferings. We must hold out through every type of weather. We need to be devoted and not shrink back after we've already begun. This is **faithfulness**.

Let me illustrate in metaphorical terms what true faith can do through a vision I once had. In God's wilderness, I was walking along the curved edge of a clear lake with a mountain ahead of me. I was a guide for some others and when I came to the mountain, it was blocking the path and left no other way to get past except to swim across the lake. I came up to the mountain and touched my finger to it and said, "Move aside." Upon saying this (words) and touching it (actions), the mountain began to crumble. Boulders tumbled down the mountainside and plunged themselves into the lake, creating a passageway where the mountain once stood.

Another illustration…The upright, children of God, are like the gems in a cold stone cave; all around is dark, cold, damp, and indistinguishable. When a flashlight or some source of light is shown on us, it's as if the Lord is piercing us with the light of holiness and it flows from the inside out so that we glow by our faith; if matched by deeds. Through God's children, His ways become loud enough to notice among the stone cold surroundings. These ways shine from us rare and precious gems, as we become guides through the uneasy terrain of low, if no, visibility around.

UNFAMILIAR

My home had been relocated, what has been and what is now are worlds apart.

The ground I tread doesn't welcome my Spirit's freshening and pure scent,

 I reach for the heavens; an imperfect white calla lily in a patch of mischievous thorns.

Oh Father, how homesick this flowing spirit inside has become!

In the flicker of a candle's flame,

 (when adoption by Love had taken me captive),

my flesh had sung lyrics of its death to this marvelous Spirit.

The ground I entered became supernatural....

LUKE 14: 27-33

What is so wonderful about coming into and remaining wholehearted towards something? Going wholeheartedly into something is being devoted to it. If one is devoted to something, he or she, to the best of their ability and if circumstances allow, intends to finish what he or she started.

In the gospel of Luke, Jesus shares a parable with His followers, saying **"Anyone who does not carry his cross and follow me cannot be my disciple. Suppose one of you wants to build a tower. Will he not first sit down and estimate the cost to see if he has enough money to complete it? For if he lays the foundation and is not able to finish it, everyone who sees it will ridicule him, saying, 'This fellow began to build and was not able to finish.' Or suppose a king is about to go to war against another king. Will he not first sit down and consider whether he is able with ten thousand men to oppose the one coming against him with twenty thousand? If he is not able he will send a delegation while the other is still a long way off and will ask for terms of peace. In the same way, any of you who does not give up everything he has cannot be my disciple" (Luke 14:27-33).** My Christ explains that it is important to go through with completely being built in him. Though, the parable does more than just show that Christ wants His treasures to finish the walk they start with Him.

The Savior is looking for one who has faith enough to say that he or she will follow and go deeper until the end, even though he or she is unsure of what a future with Him will hold. He wants them to follow no matter what uncertainties, persecution, or demands may be hiding silently around the corner. It takes <u>trust</u> to follow in such a way. Love allows us to follow in such a way, for Love always trusts **(1 Corinthians 13:7).** Keep placing rock on rock, finishing the tower that was begun until it is tall enough to exalt the King to the land and the architectural prize has come into view and in your hands.

One day, having left my grandparent's house, I came across a memorable moment. I came to a street were unique mansions line the street on either side. As the traffic light commanded me to stop, I stopped near a part of the street where two still-so-young trees grow on either sides and touch fingertips above the concrete. As I relaxed there, basking in golden waves of warmth and witnessing hazy patches of light as if enchanted, a squirrel approached the tree on the right. Running up the tree and to the top, my eyes followed as it made a daring jump one tree to the other. What inspiration that even though there was danger of cars and concrete below, the squirrel had courage and determination. It had faith that it would make it and, as a result, was able to finish the action. So must our faith be. No matter how dark the valley may lie ahead, no matter the lingering question of possible danger that will try to stop us from doing the tasks we must accomplish, we must trust the Lord fully and go all the way. That squirrel reminds me of the verse *'You will decide on a matter, and it will be established for you, and light will shine on your ways' (Job 22:28 ESV).*

An exciting moment that symbolizes trust and wholehearted faith, is found in the gospel of John. After the resurrection, Christ appears to a group of apostles who are attempting to catch some fish. Christ provides a catch of fish for them, thus revealing who he is. John writes, *'Then the disciple whom Jesus loved said to Peter, "It is the Lord!" As soon as Simon Peter heard him say, "It is the Lord," he wrapped his outer garment around him (for he had taken it off) and jumped into the water' (John 21:7).* While the others in the boat remain in it and hold on to the physical (fish), Peter leaves it all and takes a full dive to get to the Lord. No questions, no hesitation, once he learns that the Lord is waiting for him, he moves all the way.

In the parable, Jesus shares, *"For if he lays the foundation and is not able to finish it, everyone who see it will ridicule him, saying, 'This fellow began to build and was not able to finish'" (Luke 14: 29-30).* One who begins building and gives up because of the cost, is a poor example for those looking in the window of light. Consider how the hope of someone who is looking from a distance at that sturdy mountain of strength, is affected. If someone is learning how to follow and decides that it isn't worth it or that it is impossible to complete, it might be difficult for those around them who are teetering or coming in with a weak faith.

Without trusting in Christ, one will never believe that he or she can make the journey to persevere and allow their roots to grow fully into the solid foundation. My wonderful God has called me by name, knowing me personally and intimately. He knew me before anyone else (before I was born). He knows all of me. Since this is true and He made all capable of running and finishing the race to what awaits in eternity, then it can be done. The race can be finished, we can make it, and it's best to jump wholeheartedly into it! He, who is greatest, is not a liar.

By Faith not Works

Paul reasons, in a letter to the Roman believers, that *'If, in fact, Abraham was justified by works, he had something to boast about—but not before God. What does the Scripture say? "Abraham believed God and it was credited to him as righteousness." Now when a man works, his wages are not credited to him as a gift, but as an obligation. However, to the man who does not work but trusts God who justifies the wicked, his faith is credited as righteousness '(Romans 4:1-8).* Our redemption comes from faith in the Lord Jesus Christ. It comes through a personal relationship with him and not by works. If we are made righteous by our works, then the whole relationship between the Father and I would be about repayment and where is there love in it being about repayment?

The clay's opportunity to know the Potter personally is a special gift from the Potter. A gift is given as a love letter, while something given out of obligation hasn't any care attached. An obligation is more forceful than voluntary. This is contrary to love, since to give love is a choice. A true relationship is built of love, streaming through the very crevices and touching every corner. I find that working on my relationship is what matters and my works really don't carry any value or direction if I don't place my relationship as priority. If the relationship is priority and consistently built up, then all else will be made straight.

If works are given all the attention, how can anything be accomplished, since it is now only about leaning on our abilities? What happens when one can no longer accomplish what they once had? Christ informs, *"Many will say to me on that day, Lord, Lord, did we not prophesy in your name, drive out demons and perform many miracles? Then I will tell them plainly, I never knew you. Away from me, you evildoers" (Matthew 7:22-23)!* The relationship will not be created by works.

Jesus warns some of His disciples, *"However, do not rejoice that the spirits submit to you, but rejoice that your names are written in heaven" (Luke 10:20).* Precious Christ is giving a reminder that one's foundation should be built on knowing Him personally, rather than on exercised works. Do not misunderstand. It is important to know that by the Lord's power, all these remarkable things are possible, but it is intimacy with Jesus that takes first place. This will lead to a most meaningful life in Him.

Looking to Romans, it is written that *"if, in fact, Abraham was justified by works, he had something to boast about" (Romans 4:2).* This verse addresses boasting. Since we have not done the works we do on our own, we have no room to boast in ourselves. We should boast in what the Lord has done because of his love, which can only be done by knowing that Love on a deep level. David passionately proclaims, *'I will extol the Lord at all times; his praise will always be on my lips. My soul will **boast** in the Lord; let the afflicted hear and rejoice. Glorify the Lord with me; let us exalt his name together' (Psalms 34:1-3).* If it were first and foremost about works, it would be up to us to make things happen. To believe that all is about what one can do is a delusion, because precious Christ gave all things to us. Looking at our past or,' *to the rock from which you were hewn, and to the quarry from which you were dug' (Isaiah 51:1 ESV)* shows that all this goodness is from God and not from us. In that sinful nature, we were in control and all that we did was destructive. The actions were not guided by Love's light.

So in conclusion, a faith built on a foundation of works will not stand. Works above or apart from knowing my Beloved personally are worthless. Informing the Ephesians, Paul writes *'For it is by grace you have been saved, through faith—and this not from yourselves, it is the gift of God—not by works, so that no one can boast' (Ephesians 2:8-9).* This can be shown also in the fact that with non-believers, no matter how many good works they do, without knowing Christ, the works mean nothing. The person is in danger of destruction by God's wrath.

Chose Wisely What Deserves Rejoicing
[Looking into Luke 10:20]

There are multiple meanings to what my Lover was saying in Luke 10:20. As mentioned, it is important to know that by God's power and strength, I can do these works. Though, it is a relationship with God that marks a true believer and needs to be the roots that grow deep in the soil of this being; the <u>only</u> source of nutrients for sprouting roots.

Also, it is always important to remember the Lord and all that he does. As an older favorite song of mine goes, in the viewpoint of the Lord, "I remembered you, remember me." In all I do, I must give glory and thanks to my Father, for is that not what I'm here for? To bring him glory in various ways? Always be grateful for the grace he has spread over his children; we did not choose him, but he chose us and has bought us and made us free. He has called us by name. He says to me, <u>you are mine!</u>

Thirdly, if there is any boasting, boast in the Lord. Boast in what he has done, not what I have done (*'do not rejoice that the spirits submit to you'*). *"It is because of him that you are in Christ Jesus, who has become for us wisdom from God-that is, our righteousness, holiness and redemption. Therefore, as it is written: "Let him who boasts boast in the Lord (1 Corinthians 1:30-31).* I can't boast about myself even if I wanted to, because he gave all things to the rest and me.

GIVING CREDIT WHERE IT IS NEEDED

Upon entering Jerusalem, Jesus is greeted with rejoicing by his followers. He is also met with a request that the rejoicing be contained. *'Some of the Pharisees in the crowd said to Jesus, "Teacher, rebuke your disciples!" "I tell you," he replied, "If they were to keep quiet, the stones will cry out" (Luke 19:39-40).* It is hard for a human to take credit for something that is impossible by worldly understanding. It is important to understand and acknowledge that what is miraculous, what happens in the name of Christ Jesus, is not our own accomplishment or used to be given self-praise. Paul shares, *'But we have this treasure in earthen vessels, that the excellence of the power may be of God and not of us' (2 Corinthians 4:7NKJV).* We are ships carrying chests full of Christ's power. Always give credit to where it is needed, to him who deserves it.

King Herod Agrippa I failed to relinquish the praise that was rightfully the Father's and *'Immediately, because Herod did not give praise to God, an angel of the Lord struck him down, and he was eaten by worms and died' (Acts 12:23).* This happened because the people had been exclaiming that he was a god. Herod then allowed them to believe this, as he didn't allow God the praise.

Paul and Barnabas paint a more appropriate picture of not taking credit for what they did not do themselves. When Paul healed a cripple in Lystra, the people proclaimed that he and his companion were gods. *'But when the apostles Barnabas and Paul heard of this, they tore their clothes and rushed out into the crowd, shouting: "Men, why are you doing this? We too are only men, human like you. We are bringing you good news, telling you to turn from these worthless things to the living God, who made heaven and earth and sea and everything in them" (Acts 14:14-15).*

Does The Lord always respond with immediate punishment, the way he did to Herod, when someone takes praise away from Him? The Lord is love, yet he will be the judge of our lives. We should never consciously be collecting tokens that the Father is searching for. As for how the Lord will respond to someone who deliberately takes his praise; like the apostles in reverent fear, do not put the Lord to the test.

HAGGAI 1:2-6-OFFER THE FIRST FRUITS

In the book of Haggai, God speaks through His prophet concerning what was being done with His peoples' priorities. *'This is what the Lord Almighty says, 'These people say, the time has not yet come for the Lord's house to be built.' Then the word of the Lord came through the prophet Haggai: "Is it a time for you yourselves to be living in your paneled house while this house remains in ruin?" Now this is what the Lord Almighty says: Give careful thought to your ways. You have planted much but you have harvested little'* (Haggai 1:2-6). These people gave themselves the first fruits, making them unfruitful. To accomplish anything, The Master Sculptor requires our priorities to be in order, beginning with Him. He asks for our first fruits. My Lord instructed the Israelites, saying *"When you enter the land I am going to give you and reap its harvest, bring to the priest a sheaf of the first grain you harvest"* (Lev. 23:10). *"You must not eat any bread, or roasted or new grain, until the very day you bring this offering to you God. This is to be a lasting ordinance for the generations to come wherever you live"* (23:14).

As a Proverb states *'Honor the Lord with your wealth, with the first fruits of your crops: then your barns will be filled to overflowing, and your vats will brim over with new wine"* (Proverbs 3:9-10). When you examine your life, what is given the greatest amount of time? Where are the greatest efforts or most intensive searches for answers? What are your priorities and who has the top of the pyramid?

The Lord wants the best of us. Consider that we are most effective and productive when we give our best. That is what Christ wants! What is chosen first from a series of prizes when someone is given the choice? One will go for what he or she sees as the greatest on the list. Spiritual refueling daily is a must since every day we are being poured out; the way to do this is to hope in the Lord *(Isaiah 40:31)*, meditate on his words *(Psalms 1:2-3)*, and out of love, obey what he has commanded, even connect with other members of the body when possible. Satan likes to hit heavily on one's thoughts and empty space is always an invitation. Satan will hit when one is meditating on Christ. It is up to him or her to fight it with truth of scripture as Christ had when He was being tempted in the desert.

Christ is holy and perfect, so giving Him the first fruits of everything is giving it into the best hands possible. *"If the part of the dough offered as first fruits is holy, then the whole batch is holy; if the root is holy, so are the branches"* (Romans 11:16). A little yeast can work through the entire dough; if given to be made righteous, then righteousness will work in the whole body. As

I have experienced, if I give the beginning of everything by meditating, listening to him, and being still in the Lord, my whole day and whatever is presenting itself, is more accomplishable. I am able to be more hopeful and prepared to go out like a sheep among wolves. If the Lord receives the best, it will be blessed so that the whole will be beautiful.

We must make Christ our priority, otherwise it is idolatry. As Christ states, *"No one can serve two masters. Either he will hate the one and love the other, or he will be devoted to the one and despise the other. You cannot serve both God and Money" (Matthew 6:24)*. A master can be a wide range of objects and people, not restricted to money. Anything that has control or influence over one's life becomes a master. On the hike to life, there is room only for one trail guide; knowing that guide to be the Light.

Renewing or refilling the Spirit daily is a must for every morning our feet kiss the floor. What can be effective is Him first thing with our thoughts to start the day; doing something that does not take away from Christ. No other thoughts should be defeating the meditation of My Lord's words.

Haggai 1:6- First fruits of Money

"You earn wages, only to put them in a purse with holes in it" (Haggai 1:6). The money was being used towards perishable efforts. For lasting use of money, use it to build up orphanages, not palaces; building palaces were what the people around Haggai were doing, as they built up their own lifestyle, yet pushed their relationship with God to the back. Palaces show materialism, an element some have made an idol. This has only to do with the world and as the Word mentions, *'Love of the world squeezes out love for the Father. Practically everything that goes on in the world- wanting your own way, wanting everything for yourself, wanting to appear important- has nothing to do with the Father' (1 John 2:16 The Message).*

The world and all its wanting, wanting, wanting is on the way out.' But whoever does what God wants is set for eternity (1 John 2:17 Message). Building up orphanages is lasting (considering one's <u>motive,</u> for motive is just as important as act- ex. selfish gain) Using the word orphanages metaphorically, having one's focus on helping and caring for people and doing something lasting and of meaning. God says *'Love your neighbor as yourself' (Leviticus 19:18).* Solomon shares, *'A good man leaves an inheritance for his children's children, but a sinner's wealth is stored up for the righteous' (Proverbs 13:22).*

Taking up your cross Everyday

Those who take up the cross and follow, perseverant in running the race until the prize is in hand, are no longer hanging on to the bars of the standards and norms of the world. They have landed with their feet on the ground and no longer have to hang on to demands or competitions. Hanging creates sores on the hands. They are aliens who don't play in the same manner as the wicked. The Lord's children have not been afraid to let go, whether it will hurt or not, and if the distance from bars to ground is terribly far. We have died to those ways that the evil continue to play by, still holding on. *"Therefore, there is now no condemnation for those who are in Christ Jesus, because through Christ Jesus the law of the Spirit of life set me free from the law of sin and death" (Romans 8:1-2).* My Christ comes under those who are on the bars of destruction and with a compassionate nature, gently encourages them to let go because he will catch them. He will plant their feet on stable ground so they no longer hang aimlessly and immobile. Now, those who let go are able to walk away from the bars if they are perseverant and whole-heartedly ready to put both hands to the plow and not look back. They follow Christ towards the horizon that brings freedom. It is walking away with the one who has cared enough to expose the meaninglessness and unproductiveness of wasting away and loves his friends enough to help them down.

Taking up one's cross everyday, as mentioned in the Gospels of Christ, reminds me of a recent example. I felt a pull to apply for a ministry internship in Colorado. When I first discovered that it would be a year long, I became uninterested quickly and brushed it off. Unsure of what later caused a change of mind, I was suddenly filling out paperwork and sending everything for the internship. I had never been further west than Iowa, had never been out of town without someone close to me along, and had never been away from home longer than two weeks. I would unquestionably be leaving my comfort zone, family, and home town. I still applied even though I began falling victim to great fear of leaving my comfort. I was even called for an interview. It was acting in obedience, following where Christ might be moving me. I didn't get in, but I feel now that it was a test of whether or not I would follow Him into the unknown.

Taking up our crosses daily means following Jesus into the unknown, wherever he goes, no matter what it will cost, and what is left behind. What is ahead and being fought for is more lasting.

In addition, whatever one gives to the Lord, he or she will be repaid more than what was given. Consider the love that is ours, as well as the inheritance of life if we believe and have a relationship with the Lover. *"Anyone who does not take his cross and follow me is not worthy of me" (Matthew 10:38)*. We can never give The Father as much as He gives us, but we can give what we have. In doing that, we taste what an overwhelming love is given us.

Ruth discovered that unfold. Ruth left her people and town to give her time to caring for her mother-in-law, 'loving her neighbor as herself' as God commands (Read Deut. 6:1-9). She was humble, reflecting a characteristic of Jesus, who said *"I am gentle and humble in heart" (Matt. 11:29)*. She gave up the life she had to give her love away, and in doing so, God blessed her with a family, a place to stay, and even blessed her with the knowledge of who God is.

The more one follows, the deeper he is drawn into the spiritual battle. It is like a soldier walking through a storm of flying bullets or arrows as he swallows his fear, unwilling to slow his determination to reach the unmovable, unshakable, and beautiful hand that hangs extended on the opposite side of the field. The one, who extends His hand, even promises to send His Spirit to move along with the soldier. All the soldier has to do is continue moving towards the hand every day. The Shepherd won't stop watching to rest until he knows the soldier is His and safe. The Lord raises a question as He speaks *"I will bring him near and he will come close to me, for who is he who will devote himself to be close to me" (Jeremiah 30:21)?* Also, our Savior offers hope for the one who perseveres by taking his or her cross up constantly. He reveals that *"He who stands firm to the end will be saved" (Matthew 24:13)*.

Christ never promised that the road home would always be easy. Yet in scriptures, He makes it clear that it is and will be well worth it to persevere in His ways. Let's take up our crosses and move across the field and see what the Shepherd there has to offer!

~ Draw nearer to God and invite him near~

THE BEATITUDES-MATTHEW 5:3-11

Poor in Spirit- *"Blessed are the poor in spirit, for theirs is the kingdom of heaven" (Matthew 5:3).* One is in need of leaning on Jesus. One is humble and dependent on him in everything he or she does.

Mourning- *"Blessed are those who mourn, for they will be comforted" (5:4).* Humbleness is a keyword before My Father, *"For everyone who exalts himself will be humbled and he who humbles himself will be exalted" (Luke 18:14).* So, the mourning or injustice of one on earth will earn one comfort and justice in the kingdom.

Meekness- *"Blessed are the meek, for they will inherit the earth" (5:5).* Being meek is not expressing one's *own* opinions out loud but revealing the truth as the Bible reveals. Be gentle and humble in heart, carrying on Jesus' work, therefore relying on him to help achieve perfection from Him who achieved it. Lead a quiet life and be patient for the Lord.

Righteousness- *"Blessed are those who hunger and thirst for righteousness, for they will be filled" (5:6).* As a believer, when we are baptized in Christ, we are baptized into His death with Him. Given the Holy Spirit, we are being made like Christ and because of that, we will be raised from the dead like Him as well, at the resurrection. Now, the remnant have died to sin, which is in and of the world, allowing us to be raised in righteousness.

Righteousness takes perseverance. Remain morally upright. Believe the Lord and obey His commands with respectable fear. Let faithfulness be bound around our neck and written on our hearts; it should be a way of life. Many examples of righteous living can be found in the Word. Job and David share what righteousness looks like in their lives. Job wonderfully exclaims, *"I rescued the poor who cried for help and the fatherless who had none to assist him. The man who was dying blessed me; I made the widow's heart sing. I put on righteousness as my clothing; justice was my robe and my turban. I was eyes to the blind and feet to the lame. I was a father to the needy; I took up the case of the stranger. I broke the fangs of the wicked and snatched the victims from their teeth" (Job 29:12-17).* David shares, *"I do not hide your righteousness in my heart; I speak of your faithfulness and salvation. I do not conceal your love and your truth from the great assembly" (Psalms 40:10).*

*"Blessed are the **Merciful,** for they will be shown mercy" (5:7).* Looking at Christ's parable of the unmerciful servant, it reveals that to be merciful is to forgive. The Father has forgiven us and has called us to forgive. He commands, *"Freely you have received, freely give" (Matthew 10:8).* The servant, who did not have mercy on the other, was handed over to be tortured. Canceling one's 'debt' of unforgiving does not mean building anger up inside or holding grudges. If one is trying to hold people hostage by not forgiving them (you are really holding yourself hostage), they are held back from truth. If the one who is not forgiven is an unbeliever or teetering on the edge of life and death, it could be holding them from eternal life because the Father's ways are not being shown. People want to see life in action; it is confusing and ineffective to others if words and actions are not matching each other. The desire of pleasing the Lord should be enough to let go of dark pride.

Pure in Heart- *"Blessed are the pure in heart, for they will see God" (5:8).* This means not deceiving---purely innocent intentions—no acts generated and driven by revenge, etc. Wickedness is not lurking behind a veil of false righteousness.

*"Blessed are the **Peacemakers**, for they will be called sons of God" (5:9).* Many times in the Word, we are warned not to take part in quarrelling. Arguing is certainly not creating peace, but is time consuming, pointless, and can be dangerous. We are called to be peacemakers; even around our enemies. *"If your enemy is hungry, give him food to eat; if he is thirsty, give him water to drink. In doing this, you will heap burning coals on his head, and the Lord will reward you" (Proverbs 25:21-22).* As Solomon reveals, *"When a man's ways are pleasing to the Lord, he makes even his enemies live at peace with him" (Proverbs 16:7).*

*"Blessed are those who are **persecuted** because of righteousness, for theirs is the kingdom of heaven" (5:11).* Take up your cross daily, even when it seems too heavy to carry. There are unseen hands holding it up with you from the first step you took carrying it to now and all your days.

*Blessed are you when people **insult** you, **persecute** you and **falsely say all kinds of evil against you because of me.** Rejoice and be glad, because great is your reward in heaven, for in the same way they persecuted the prophets who were before you" (5:11-12).* You are free from worldly standards and norms and free to be in the joy of the Spirit. Do what is righteous and pure, even when it isn't 'normal' in others' minds.

THE TRADING OF ARMOR

When we die to sin and are being raised in righteousness, we recognize that the Lord's way is the only one that can lead us to life. Sin flows in carnal veins; flesh is of the world; the world is sin and death because it drinks and becomes drunk on Satan's persuasions. We die to the sin because we crucify sin on the cross. We nail the old 'armor' with Christ Jesus, with whom newness is made possible.

New life takes place within the once decaying wasteland of our bodies. The tornado of sin once ravaged the now virgin land, but will no more disperse every delicate flower into its violent winds.

The Holy Spirit takes over and builds as the Lord works in us; building up a temple and dwelling place. *"Don't you know that you yourselves are God's temple and that God's Spirit lives in you? If anyone destroys God's temple, God will destroy him, for God's temple is sacred, and you are that temple" (1 Cor. 3:16-17).* The Spirit of God is the source of life now, for true followers long for righteousness and work to be submissive to let the Spirit have free range in this life. It is not our own. The Father is in Christ, Christ is in us, so the Father is in us and the Spirit is of Him. One being with three parts is inside.

We who are the remnant are raised from sin to righteousness as long as we remain in the vine. How blessed we are to be saved from the coming wrath. It would be a terribly unfortunate time to have to anticipate because each day every one of us commits much sin in our lives and it builds on our records. Thankfully, Jesus was given and the ones who answer God's call are caught in the arms of freely given grace. The weighty records are shredded. *'[If] every violation and disobedience received it's just punishment, how shall we escape if we ignore such a great salvation' (Hebrews 2:2-3).* Oh how much disaster and unthinkable torture we've been pardoned from!

Spiritual death and rising

We as believers, when baptized in Christ, are baptized into his death with him. Given the Holy Spirit, who is in him as well, we are being made like him and for that reason, we will be raised from the dead like him as well; the resurrection. Now, the remnant has died to sin which is in the world and of it, allowing for the remnant to be raised in righteousness.

The Group of Believers

THE TRUE BODY

The Church is not a physical building but, as modeled in the New Testament, a body of believers striving to glorify the Lord. We gather, encourage, instruct in the word and rebuke (when needed) one another in fellowship and carry on a building of the body with our unique spiritually manifested gifts.

Sometimes the church misses the idea in which the greatness and glory of God is shown to the world by how brothers and sisters in Christ treat one another; to show Christ's love to one another. As I have come to experience, there are arguments and siblings avoiding one another due to divisions of beliefs. These beliefs surround denominations. Labels often enter into pointless religion.

How can Christ's body function if the parts are at odds? On earth, my Christ explained that 'if Satan drives out Satan, Satan cannot stand, he is divided, like with a divided house. If the house is divided, then it cannot stand' *(referred to in Matthew 12:25-27).* Jesus is trying to communicate that if His friends are against one another, they have allowed the enemy a victory. Paul criticizes the Corinthians for quarrelling by writing, *'One brother goes to law against another-and this in front of unbelievers! The very fact that you have lawsuits among you means you have been completely defeated already' (1 Corinthians 6:6:7).*

When discussing my faith with a coworker, this person had mentioned her family being divided in beliefs in debatable matters. The way some of the family members thought was very different from others and as a result they could no longer speak about their faith, just to keep the peace. Jesus prays *"May [future believers] be brought to complete unity to let the world know that you sent me and have loved them even as you have loved me (John 17:23).* If believers are constantly in discord, those who are looking in Christ's window may look at the divisions and consider passing by. If they have been informed that Christ is Love, they might wonder why we are in constant discord. If Christ would make efforts to avoid discord with those on His team, then why shouldn't we?

When I was younger, living in my childhood home, my good friend's mother would have others gather with her in her living room as they lit candles and joined together in peace. The difference from my friend's mother's faith gatherings and some church meetings today is that genuine fellowship and working together are stolen from the latter. For many, focus becomes strictly on the pastor and not much other than a greeting is sent between strangers, leaving some who attend uncomfortable. Demonstrated love is the only way the church can truly function in the way Christ designed it to. Love is the bonding agent that holds the Beautiful Body together, whistling through every space between the joints.

If we all work on love, myself included, Solomon writes *'When a man's ways are pleasing to the LORD, he makes even his enemies live at peace with him'* (Proverbs 16:7). Though true siblings in Christ are not enemies, love will have a result like that of this Proverb. If all focused on Christ's love and consistently asked for his help as we strive to imitate his actions and treat people with love and compassion, then we could all get along and make this body function!

The Remnant of the Lord

In Christ's parable of the wedding banquet, told in *Matthew 22,* those who were first invited to come were the people of Israel. Now throughout history, even in Moses' time, the natural descendents constantly turned from the The Potter's love (forty years in the desert). They did not deserve to come because they did not take hold of the Father's invitation to life. Even today, there are those of this decent who do not believe that Christ is who He says He is, that He returned to life, or that He offers life.

When the servants from this parable go to invite anyone, they invite *"others"*. These others were the ones who were predestined to be adopted into the family of God. The Lord reveals, *"I have other sheep that are not of this sheep pen. I must bring them also" (John 10:16).* Jesus Christ invited others to come to join the Father at His table. Those who were adopted now had room to come in, find life, and be declared safe in the presence of this King. *"Some of the branches have been broken off, and you, though a wild olive shoot, have been grafted in among the others and now share in the nourishing sap from the olive root" (Romans 11:17).* There is an invitation to find a friend and beloved if we come and consistently remain in Him. He has allowed all reconciliation with an undeserved God. Also, the ones who are adopted and not of natural descent are no less loved, because as Paul shares, *"God does not show favoritism" (Romans 2:11).*

Jesus was the word made flesh, coming down from the throne of heaven to bring the lost sheep to Himself and His everlasting pasture. At the crucifying of the Lord, He made Himself an eternal sin offering for the true seeds, which are the remnant. He used His blood to wash us clean of the old clothes in which scripture warns, *'you were taught, with regard to your former way of life, to put off your old self, which is being corrupted by its deceitful desires" (Ephesians 4:22).*

The true seeds are the ones who embrace the call, coming for life in the Lord Jesus Christ. The seeds are scattered on all corners of the earth. The remnant recognizes that they have been shown much mercy and have been blessed beyond the curse. Just because one is a natural descendant of Abraham, doesn't mean that they are part of the promise. *'For not all who are descended from Israel are Israel. Nor because they are his descendants are they all Abraham's children. On the contrary, "It is through Isaac that your offspring will be reckoned." In other words, it is not the natural children who are God's children, but it is the children of the promise who are regarded as Abraham's offspring (Romans 9:6-8).* The true seeds are the church, which are the body of Christ. Not an actual place or race, but the parts that make up the body of Christ.

How beautiful and generous to receive and invitation from the Lord. How wonderful to a part of the wedding banquet, where there is room for all who, instead of setting the invitation aside to be misplaced, rsvp right away. We will by no means find it a waste of time. When the day of the wedding banquet comes, we will find it well worth it. So, don't fall away!

Trees of Life

Unintentional departure, falling on different grounds.
A blessed few seeds find the satisfying fertile soil,
Drinking up the abundant living water that continuously flows,
Unfailing and non-discriminate accessibility;
The roots are growing.
My Love, let my roots grow deeper into the fertile soil of this heart
And let your roots damage and choke the insecurity and dark sprouts,
whose beginnings may lurk just beneath the surface.
Invade those that have reached the surface to multiply.
Your roots of spiritual growth conquer by wrapping around and cutting
off their life supply,
To make room for a thick tree (representing strength in your mighty
hands);
Unparalleled in size (for your domination in this life no longer my own),
And magnificent beyond any inspiration (faith is precious; Christ is a
precious gift).
Each leaf holds a masterpiece of ways I take up my cross daily and follow
him.
So long a wait, it seems, but if these roots persistently push through the
moist soil to find the streams nearby;*
What rare, succulent, and treasured fruit will find its place along the
branches; surrounded by their dense layers of leaves.
Behold, fruit pleasing to My King.

*'But his delight is in the law of the Lord, and on his law he meditates day
and night. He is like a tree planted by streams of water, which yields its
fruit in season and whose leaves do not wither. Whatever he does prospers'
(Psalms 1:2-3).

UNPARALLEL

Adoption is starting a new life, a new family, and a new house. It is being wiped clean of old routines.

In our days of destruction, we were sons and daughters of Satan. *'This is how we know who the children of God are and who the children of the devil are: Anyone who does not do what is right is not a child of God; nor is anyone who does not love his brother' (1 John 3:10).* When we under Satan's control, we do not know love because there is no love in him. We cannot give love away when we have none to give. Our former father encourages us in evil, to drown in our desires and be sold to temptation. Only one who is very uncaring could support such deeds and behavior.

When a child is in an abusive home and it is discovered, they are taken from that corruption. A loving father will discipline so that his child may grow and move beyond the original heights to greater ones. The Loving Father God adopts us by His grace so that we may have the chance to be given a new life. When we are right, He smiles on us. When we are wrong, He disciplines us so we may learn from our mistakes and can better strive in spirit towards the goal of perfection in Christ. By His will, He has taken His chosen ones from the old and adopted us into his family, where we may learn love and have an unimaginable new beginning and purpose!

Praise--No One Compares to Him

CREEK SIDE APPRECIATION

Left and right, flora's hands open wide to say she will fight for her innocence this much;
As far as her boundaries reach.
A puff of fragrance from a hidden location reveals the smell of roses.
Fresh petals dance with a spin at summer's finale.
The water passing through carries a golden coin appearance,
As the aquatic plants that wave below the creek's surface show off their most vibrant shade,
To pierce through the water.
Like the working of an old music box,
Dots of white foam are sent down the rapid creek, randomly placed.
The line of trees along the golden mirror, bow their heads at different degrees,
As I return the bow to send a silent greeting.
The trees forever bow in respect
As my voice echoes through the corner of beauty,
Nestled in the midst of creation.

LORD OF MIRACLES

He rides across cotton puffs,
On anything that shows high rank.
A savannah hued sun burst of rays,
to contribute to his already glorified image.
He calls down and the lightning strikes in the field.
The sight is like moonlight through Ice caves.
Maybe it resembles a camera's flash.
The lightning slips through the places of brokenness in the line of still
visible clouds.
He weaves the unlikely and composes the unnatural.
He emphasizes that the world's boundaries are too confined.
We are placed under this painted dome,
Animated by Artist and glorified Inventor.
We have sight to see the clouds chase clouds across the day
and the celestial guards riding across the night.
Surely He is watching and His presence draws near,
to fan the flames of this holy fire.
Near enough to finger through the mystery of these spoken tongues.
He grants wonderful joys and taps into the confidence that the attitude of
being 'impossible' doesn't exist.
You never fail to go beyond what has been established in the minds of
men.

*~I saw heaven standing open and there before me was a white horse, whose
rider is called Faithful and True. With justice he judges and makes war.
His eyes are like blazing fire, and on his head are many crowns. He has
a name written on him that no one knows but he himself. He is dressed
in a robe dipped in blood, and his name is the Word of God. The armies
of heaven were following him, riding on white horses and dressed in fine
linen, white and clean. Out of his mouth comes a sharp sword with which
to strike down the nations. "He will rule them with an iron scepter." He
treads the winepress of the fury of the wrath of God Almighty. On his robe
and on his thigh he has this name written: King of Kings and Lord of Lords.
(Revelation 19:11-16)~*

Malachi 3-Demonstration of Generosity and Compassion

Savior, throughout history, has been generous in offerings to lavish His children with love. *"Ever since the time of your forefathers you have turned away from my decrees and have not kept them. Return to me, and I will return to you," says the Lord Almighty'* (Malachi 3:7). My Christ certainly puts up with much. His creations have turned away so many times, but are always offered another chance. They have been forgiven every time that they return to Him. Savior is always willing to take us back, despite the mistakes that have weaved through our web of actions. As long as The Day or death hasn't come, it is never too late to mend and reconcile the relationship we have with the Father.

One day I considered how rejection must feel for my Lord. I thought, even though he can surely take rejection better than I, how he must feel for enduring much rejection from his own creations. Many reject the gifts meant for them. They reject what my Christ, as our Sculptor, knows we need. He knows that what He offers will rescue us from a life of tears and misery. Jesus was rejected by 'friends' and many others. By His own will, He allowed them to send him out of the world. Christ was and is offering life, which is given out of love. All my stories of rejection don't quite compare, seeming so small against Christ's great testimony of betrayal.

A minor story of mine is a very faint example of Christ's story. Out of love, I gave my little sister some horses that I really believed she would like. She enjoys collecting horses to record short videos and I was excited to give her these gifts. She decided to get rid of many of the nice horses because they weren't the 'brand' she wanted to collect. I was upset because she didn't accept what I had made available for her. I didn't have as much a desire to give her more after that, but I continue to every once in a while anyways, just in case she accepts it.

As humans we may not understand why Savior is so generous, especially when it is sometimes hard for us to be generous ourselves. As my Christ informs, *"My thoughts are not your thoughts neither are your ways my ways, as the heavens are higher than the earth, so are my ways higher than your ways and my thoughts than your thoughts"* (Isaiah 55: 8-9). Humans aren't perfect and sometimes it seems humans lack mercy and forgiveness on those who make mistakes; sometimes giving up on them. My Christ's Word also informs us, *'The Lord does not look at the things man looks at.*

Man looks at the outward appearance, but God looks at the heart' (1 Samuel 16:7). We are so blessed that Savior does not look at us the way we have looked at each other! It would be harsh because I know all of us have given harsh judgments of another person before.

We are blessed also when it is said, *"I the Lord do not change. So you, O descendants of Jacob, are not destroyed"* (Malachi 3:6). He does not change His mind about forgiving us, accepting us despite our flaws, or generously offering us wonderful gifts!

My Christ never lets go. He gives freely and generously because He wants every part of us; our love and obedience. Jesus said, *"My yoke is easy and my burden is light"* (Matthew 11:30). Authority and every great thing are being held out in his hands.

Every day, my Christ offers a new morning as a demonstration of His great love, kindness, and generosity. If one is quiet and reflects, they can find a ton more ways that Christ has been generous! Receive what he is so generously offering. *'Then those who feared the Lord talked with each other, and the Lord listened and heard. A scroll of remembrance was written in his presence concerning those who feared the Lord and honored his name. They will be mine, says the Lord Almighty. In the day when I make up my treasured possession, I will spare them, just as in compassion a man spares his son who serves him. And you will again see the distinction between the righteous and the wicked, between those who serve God and those who do not'* (Malachi 3:16-18).

Jesus' Love Chronicle—My Song of Songs

He is a melodic song I sing everyday.

It gets hard to contain the desire to see his hope streaming face.

Those eyes are like a myth come true,

I just can't stop looking again to make sure mine aren't fooling me.

A movement in his takes the focus off of all life on the other side of these imitation mirrors.

I can't ignore this forever admiration that engulfs the environment between us; that he has for me and I for him.

That aura of protection that ripples out the fear,

sending it to dock elsewhere.

I know he treasures faithfulness to me because he truly cares,

Anything he'd do to give life to these intriguing dances every glorious day.

Why is it when we steal an embrace, a once stalking loneliness is exiled and the arms holding me captive won't weaken for the ages.

He leads me on an adventure to territory outside the borders of dullness.

Oh that smile of his; the reaction to a positive experiment where I seek my cure in it.

The desires circulating in my spirit surpass the perception this world has of love, in truth and innocence, for they do not overstep into the fiery realm.

Rest your arm across my shoulder again, I wonder if you feel the chills of an overwhelming peace and for that moment, tomorrow's worries can consume themselves.

His hand once again pushes my strands of hair away from my cheek and falls down it like paint down glass.

A Psalm-Take Me

Father how you hold me back from the state of disrepair.
You are my sword against the hostility from the enemy's fortress.
What purity is entwined in my voice that you lean near to listen to all
that I say?
Mix the purest ingredients
and make the perfect remedy at your precise time,
before the trap door appears and opens under me.
Before thorns surface and erupt into many down the trail.
You reassure me that I belong to you,
 Not the source of darkness,
For what I have done that has been distasteful to you,
Do turnarounds and become what you want them to be.

REVELATION

I must have been in a trance; a little dizzy and leaving all voices and sights behind for an amount of time. I had revealed to me a vision of brilliant colors. Spread was a navy sky of still visible light blue clouds filling it and they seemed so close. In the center came two enormous hands that pulled apart the sky, making a circular opening in it and revealing a day-like light that contrasted greatly from the original shady hues. Two lines of angels on both sides of the hands in the opening were grabbing onto and pulling back two lines of clouds as if they were ribbons. As that happened, the night clouds that dominated the rest of the sky (many were over buildings/ the town) fled from the hands and the opening. Meanwhile, on the ground were various man-made structures. By the touch of the light from the opening, every structure dissolved. They were blown away like the aged dandelion being dispersed into the wind. It was magnificent to witness as I came back to someone's voice calling for my attention.

SHADES AND SHADOWS

Echoes of the natives whispering through my ears,
The calls of wild animals with every forgoing step I set.
The cliffs are like waves in the sea after an angering fight with the storms,
Waterfalls like soft hanging hair,
Waiting for hands to string through it like a harp.
Have we come here to be small in so much greatness?
All around us like the sparkling spider webs of dew?
The cliffs streaming springs compose a peaceful softness that calms my uneasiness
From the chaos lying beyond this wonderful display.
Who are we to take a simple passing glance,
at a masterpiece by the talents of my King?
A genius in details and brilliant in color.

SONG FOR THE SON

I feel my eyes lit with a glow as I come to know what a day of Your peace and rest are like.

The hate dissolved,

The need is felt, to twist and shatter the worldly fear that presses on every side.

Shaken through the sifter, of the One who restores, were the polluted waters of the pools in the eyes; now cleansed to waves of innocence.

Memories only return as tools that help reach another hand.

Song for the Son, give me a lifetime in Your unbound sky of pure love; where Your Spirit consumes me, colliding with and ripping through the center of the portrait of the old.

Oh Love, a lifetime in Your arms is where I belong.

Allow me to see how You have seen and felt,

 as You gaze intently over the grounds every moment,

 for I desire to imitate my Love's ways.

In the shadow's momentary cover, stretch Your arms well into the breath overhead to lift me so high,

as gravity throws a lasso around my burdens.

Falling under me, the burdens are crushed under Your holy feet,

 as the cornerstone that crushes the wicked.

With the loss of that unwanted weight, I may lift the sword and set it against the fear overtaking the land.

Please let me borrow Your courage so that I may stand on this height that is above all intimidation and triumph as You have promised.

At my side, You always whisper renewal and reconstruction;

Mysteriously, the sweetness of Your voice transfers to the strength of my cape of faith.

You enfold me always and allow me to ride on wings of great understanding in You.

Our bond will always run deeper than the bones well submerged in my skin.

PROTECTION AND STRENGTH

I always see opportunities in many situations that my Beloved brings my way, for everything happens for a reason and I am an instrument of the Holy One. I am a holder of the word of truth and an agent of change. Without my Christ, I am weak and fearful. But with his protection and strength I am prepared to kick the demonic forces out from where they don't belong and face persecution with boldness. I walk fearless among them.

Insight that my Lord has given me is about a sand hill and a sturdy mountain; by myself, I am a sand hill which is washed away by the waves of life's crookedness. With Christ, I am a sturdy mountain in which the water can never erode the foundation, since it is layered with the protective Rock. I am shielded from erosion.

The only true strength and protecting power is in him; not found in anything else. *"O LORD God Almighty, who is like you? You are mighty, O LORD, and your faithfulness surrounds you' (Psalms 89:8).* My Lord is mighty, protecting, and faithful to the child who relies on Him and does His will by obeying His commands.

I had a dream that addressed the importance of leaning on the impenetrable tower, Christ, and holding to His commands. In simplicity, it showed that spiritual strength and protection, from worldly destruction, is available when I depend on Christ. The dream revealed two trucks that were parked one in front of the other. The rear bumper of one was not too far from the front bumper of the other. Neither was moving, which caused me to assume they wouldn't collide. My hand was resting on the rear bumper, in between the two. Suddenly, the other truck darted toward the one in front of it. It seemed my hand was about to face its doom. Suddenly, a bible appeared in my hand and somehow allowed my hand to dodge the disaster that would have crushed the body part beyond repair. I came to understand that my hand was really a substitution for myself. The bible was a metaphor of God's loving protection and strength in His Word, which applies to any situation that I may face.

Obedience in what the Word says (Coming to and believing Christ) and standing in His light, creates a shield of protection that allows us to never be destroyed. *'Wait for his Son from heaven, whom he raised from the dead-Jesus, who rescues us from the coming wrath' (1 Thessalonians 1:10).* The choice to take our generously given chance at salvation leaves us able to lay down our fear at the foot of the mountain and, in His strength, climb! In His protection, we don't have to worry about being crushed or lost!

YOUR WORKS, MY LOVE, ARE ALWAYS IN MOTION

How wonderful is the Lord. Christ came down as the bread from heaven, to eat a meal with and hold hands with his creations. How many ancient false gods have been said to do such things? In the time that the Great Light had walked the earth as flesh, many, instead of embracing the privilege of the company of this miracle, persecuted Him. He was often persecuted for doing what was, in the sight of those who recognized the Father, wonderful. However, the wonders he displayed were unacceptable to those who followed pointless manmade laws. These included multiple actions that were unlawful for a Sabbath. *'So, because Jesus was doing these things on the Sabbath, the Jews persecuted him. Jesus said to them, "My Father is always at his work to this very day, and I, too, am working" (John 5:16).* Jesus said this because under no man's schedule or tradition can the Holy Spirit, what is from and of the Father, be restrained. The Father does what he pleases with his Spirit and the children who bear that Spirit (and are submissive).

"The wind blows wherever it pleases. You hear its sound, but you cannot tell where it comes from or where it is going. So it is with everyone born of the Spirit" (John 3:8). Like the wind, who can grasp the Holy Spirit in their hands and control His movement? Who can make it be still? By the Holy Spirit, the warriors that are The Father's possessions are always changing and maturing, if faithful and perseverant in spiritual walk. We are always changing so that our actions match words. We are changed so that we may serve, teach, and live as a testimony to others.

People begin believing when the message of Christ is revealed, so the work of the Father is always in motion. The results of God's work are constantly active as long as someone is willing to obey and follow.

My love is truly always at work because even the unchangeable truth, by no form of darkness and lie, can be hidden. *'For whatever is hidden is meant to be disclosed, and whatever is concealed is meant to be brought out into the open' (Mark 4:22).* The light of Holiness and truth cannot be silenced, for the Lord is not one who settles in containment; by no means! *'The heavens, even the highest heavens cannot contain you' (2 Chronicles 6:18).* Since the Father cannot be contained, he is not limited in ways he can make Himself and all truth known. Luke shares that *'Some of the Pharisees in the crowd said to Jesus, "Teacher, rebuke your disciples!" "I tell you," he* replied, *"If they were to keep quiet, the stones will cry out" (Luke 19:39-40).* The Lord is able to make anything unnatural and natural to reveal His immeasurable power; pulling up truth, so it won't be cloaked.

Recall the corrupted prophet Balaam. When the truth went unnoticed, his donkey proclaimed it. Sometimes it seems that the enemy has attempted to restrain or silence the truth of God's work in many ways. When listening to reason has been refused, from somewhere and at any moment, it will be proclaimed.

The Father can always find someone who has their hands in the air reminding him "Here am I, Lord send me!" They will become a witness for the Father and bring glory to Him. The wonders that are done through that faithful worker can be a witness to reveal The Father to other hearts. Thus the work of His Spirit continues.

Being Prepared

IN AND OUT OF SEASON- ALWAYS PREPARED

In 2 Timothy, Paul includes the instruction to *"Preach the word; be prepared in season and out of season; correct, rebuke, and encourage with great patience and careful instruction" (4:2).* This idea of being in and out of season is that a child of God needs to be prepared to work in the harvest field at any time. This means being willing to act in times when it is convenient or inconvenient for us. At random, we may need to respond to someone who is parched and thirsty for the living water of Christ. To do so, we should be alert and prepared for this or any other movement the Lord chooses to make.

An example was late one night when I was checking my email. Rather tired and intending on going to bed very soon, I was ready to get off just as an acquaintance started a conversation. He began opening up to me for the first time about an unfortunate addiction he had been struggling with. Later, he thanked me. I assume for being there to listen and support. It was an inconvenient moment for me since it was late, I was tired, and I had to get up early in the morning for work. With great patience, I welcomed the moment, being open to the possibility that the Lord just might have brought this situation to me for a reason; that He might want to work in it. I remained open to support him in the Lord.

Everything happens for a reason. We must always be prepared, especially since it is the Father's will. Remember, the sweet Father owns our lives, for we are no longer our own and how blessed we are for that! When His grace brought new life, we grab onto it, confessing that we no longer want to be in control of our lives. We know that His ways are the only escape from death. We know that when He is able to work in a situation, things are accomplished. We are on His schedule, He is not on ours. Our time is for His purpose.

There is a time when certain things such as fruit grow. There is a period when it is juicy, delicious, and at its best stage, like blueberries are in summer. If something is out of season, it is not its best quality, attracting less people; it may be less productive. This can be so in different seasons of our faith. We may not be as productive out of season as we are in season, but don't let that be a hindrance or excuse for being unprepared! If there is a pop quiz and one does not know the class material, the result should be less accuracy and a low grade. If there is a building project planned, yet everyone forgets their tools, what can be accomplished? But if we are always prepared wherever we go, how much can be accomplished! It is important to remain on the foundation of our relationship with the Father in heaven and staying sharpened in the spiritual gifts we've been given.

⸺ ⸺

No Thief in the Night-I
Thessalonians 5:2

To the Thessalonians, Paul writes *'For you know very well that the day of the Lord will come like a thief in the night' (1 Thessalonians 5:2).* For an unbeliever who lives in the night, the true greatness of what is revealed through Christ is concealed because they are not being led by light. Jesus is the light of the world. Whoever follows Him will never walk alone and in darkness, because they have the light of life. *'The light shines in the darkness, but the darkness has not understood it' (John 1:5).* If the darkness has not understood the light, and the world lives in darkness, then the world will not know how to respond to it. Confusion hinders a person from being prepared with an appropriate physical or mental response; not expecting a change at all. *"Therefore keep watch, because you do not know on what day your Lord will come. But understand this: If the owner of the house had known at what time of night the thief was coming, he would have kept watch and would not have let his house be broken into. So you also must be ready, because the Son of Man will come at an hour when you do not expect him" (Matthew 24:42-43).*

In Matthew twenty-five, the end days are compared to ten virgins who are awaiting the arrival of the bridegroom. Five are wise while the other five are foolish. The wise ones bring extra oil in jars for the lamps they are carrying. The foolish ones do not and before the groom arrives, they have to go back to get some oil for their dying lamps. Only the wise are allowed to enter His chambers with Him.

Like the wise virgins with oil who were prepared, everything will be clear and revealed. The children of God are of day and light; the light of day carries an exposing effect and all is revealed that is set to the light. Jesus, being the *'friend that sticks closer than a brother' (Proverbs 18:24),* has been pleased to share knowledge of what will come to his friends. A person shares everything with a true friend.

For Christ to share what He knows and make things clear, we must always be awake in our faith. We must be prepared. The extra oil in jars is like studying the Word, understanding what it is saying, and living it out in life. If a believer does not know what The Bible says, how can he or she truly know who Christ is or what He wants with us? How can one remain living in freedom from captivity? Most importantly, how can one build his or her relationship with Him and be prepared? Ask Him for understanding or what your faith is lacking. *"The prayer of a righteous man is powerful and effective" (James 5:16).* When His beloved speaks, Christ leans near to listen.

Understanding is important to be able to live out our faith. Living it is very important, since faith without deeds is dead (Read James 1:22-25, 2:14-26). One cannot lead others out of darkness with a light source that isn't lit. The wise virgins were strangers in a strange land, who could identify the groom because they knew His plans and how He warned to be prepared. They had nothing to worry about because they used their time wisely to get oil; living life for the Lord. Their lamps had enough oil to keep burning. Our faith must be strong enough to last.

Jesus stated that His sheep know His voice, they follow Him, and He knows them; their eyes are trained to identify His overwhelming light. In relation to coming to the right voice, we can be prepared by putting on the armor of truth, so that *'at that time, if anyone says to us, "look, here is the Christ!" or "There he is' (Matthew 24:23),* you won't believe it, for Christ's words will have been fulfilled and the spirit of truth will confirm. No one should have to tell us when the end has come! In Jesus' words, the vultures gather where the body is (reference Matthew 24:28). *"Since we belong to the day, let us be self-controlled, putting on faith and love as a breastplate, and the hope of salvation as a helmet. For God did not appoint us to suffer wrath but to receive salvation through our Lord Jesus Christ. He died for us so that, whether we are awake or asleep, we may live together with him" (1 Thessalonians 5:8-10).*

PLACE OF PEACE

Swept landscape,
Folded wings
Clouds drifting by beyond the ground.
Morning mist,
Drops of dew.
The flowers are anew.
Kneeling in prayers
and crouching in the light.
Receiving the echoes of water,
 trickling over the surfaces of blue stones.
The joy redoubled, advancing, invading;
Not enclosed and not concealed.
From the chaos that presses on every side, there is always an escape.
Holding this key to eternity,
Protection, through the hush, surrounds like the light of a candle.
Strength built.
Reassurance of love; welling up.
Glad to come and meet with you again, Lord.

"Come with me by yourselves to a quiet place and get some rest" ~Mark 6:31

Help

You'll Show Me Love

I see Him as beautiful and the inspiration,
A glimpse of somewhere deeply longed for.
He is the country scent of harvest time,
Comfort telling me I am worthy of love.
His hands are not hesitant or afraid to help me into the warmth of light.
He owns the voice that rescues me from this mocking prison,
And is the sunset that I want to stare at long enough to make all else fade.
His breath is in the approaching summer dusk,
And the leafy whirlwinds that dance among autumn.
He is the artist shaping His unique treasure and signing His name in me,
 to claim what He has delighted in claiming.
I Am Worthy of Love, even when I don't believe, the spirit does and the Father knows that worth;
He calls from the fields of my heart for me to find my worth.
Teach me again please, for I have fallen into the fierce waves and need that hand to reach for me
Christ my brother, my Love.

"I Will Reach for You, Oh Keeper of My Love; the Fresh Ground of My Garden; Seed of The Good Soil, Lover of My Sight; YOU Are Worthy Of Love" -Christ

A Psalm-Transition Fear to Joy

Lord, how my feelings deceive me and seem to be used against me to try to lead me astray.

Today I fall at my knees to beg you to lead me away from falling into temptation, believing what I shouldn't be in relation to what I know in You.

Let me fight this that cannot be trusted.

In mind, the devil creeps up, threatening my thoughts with the prospect of a supposed fate in hell.

As if that were possible! That I am refuse to my God

Such a theory will never hold a note of truth to save Satan's life!

I cry as my face is buried in my arms and my hands dig at the fibers of my chocolate carpet.

Find me peace, oh Lord, oh so soon, hurry and show me your hope enduring beauty!

I'm cut with distress right now.

But your word is not far from my reach and I open it to find a common ground with a great warrior of God, in the poetic language of Psalms;

It speaks to me.

My crying turns to peace amidst the words of the Holy Scriptures.

I am safe; I am comforted, and I want to praise God!

~Your righteousness, O God, reaches to the highest heavens. You have done such wonderful things. Who can compare with you, O God? You have allowed me to suffer much hardship, but you will restore me to life again and lift me up from the depths of the earth. You will restore me to even greater honor and comfort me once again (Psalms 71:19-21 NLT) ~

I want to thank you Father for allowing me to enter peace and rest and not allowing me to finish because of those sudden laughing fits that make evident my victory, generated from your operation within. Not just one day have I heard your love and kindness, but I have heard it everyday; you have given it every morning. I just can't live by what I feel. Rather, allow me to always live by the truth of everything. Feelings, as proven over and over again, are deceiving; a guide eager to lead this traveler astray.

In the name of great power, Jesus

Amen

FATHER OF RESCUE

Father, may I follow you?
I admire what you are.
This path home is rather rugged
and splattered in random places with unpleasant tar.
Reach for me and I can make it through them;
To a clean space I can sometimes get.
Father whatever would I do if you I had never accepted?
A sweet smell sweeps across my nose;
You planted me delicate flowers, made by your dexterous hands.
But a door is near with an enemy's voice;
Please help me secure the latch.
Beyond the flowers demonic eyes stare to poison me so,
They wait impatiently for me to be polluted by the contamination they
emit.
I believe a boat is approaching, an illuminate one for sure;
It's my Father the Lord, here to rescue me.
He helps me onto the vessel and we sail on a sea so pure.
The distance reveals a distinctive palace, where love is set in stone.
Inside my Father's throne welcomes Him,
And exposes a magnificence one has never known.
Now inside I am asked to accept the laws and rules of the King.
I accept and am presented as the princess.
Excitement takes me over and before my Father I sing.
He walks me to the purity-trimmed window and asks me what I see.
I glance out far across the land
As I tell my Father that the darkness that poisoned has fully died out.
He whispers, "Now you are Free."

PRAYER FOR REJUVENATION

Shine Lord when the sickness of hopelessness strikes,
Arise in my heart, arise Spirit.
Reveal yourself when the will to persevere dies and it refuses to be revived
to full life again.
Support my body when oppressing winds blow truth from under me.
Stream my spirit with beautiful words when temptation's sword threatens
to cut me too deep.
Grip me with thoughts of undisturbed places of rest and a narrow path
littered with inspiration.
Yet splatter some of it with the mess of persecution as it inspires as well to
remind me that the spiritual battle has long been conceived and raging.
Fierce rumbles erupt between the army of righteousness and of darkness.
Remind me somehow, that you the Holy Father never stop using us,
*For you just need to play your instruments in order to make the song
perfect.

~'Therefore we do not lose heart. Though outwardly we are wasting
away, yet inwardly we are being renewed day by day' (2 Corinthians
4:16) ~

* *The Lord shared this with me on the drive to work one morning, saying that
The Lord never stops using us; He just has to play His instruments in order so
that the song will be perfect.'*

I always enjoy hearing testimony of how the Lord is working in small or great ways. I would enjoy hearing whatever testimony you are willing to share…so write or email me with any stories. Who knows? I might even ask to use it anonymously as an example in future topic papers.

~~~~~~~~~~~

~Also, a thanks to Bradley, Carrie, and Elizabeth for help with editing on this project~

NOTES